THE
BIG BOOK
OF OIL
PAINTING

The history, the studio, the materials
the techniques, the subjects, the theory
and the practice of oil painting

by
JOSÉ M. PARRAMÓN

Parramón editions

Published by Parramón Ediciones, S.A.
Lepanto, 264, 4.º - Barcelona - (Spain)

© José M.ª Parramón Vilasaló

Register Book Number: 785
Legal Deposit: 26075-1983
ISBN: 0-86343-031-7

Printed in Spain by
Printer Industria Gráfica, S.A.
Provenza, 388 Barcelona-25

Distributed in United Kingdom by
FOUNTAIN PRESS LTD.
65, Victoria Street,
Windsor, Berkshire SL41EH

Painting and Drawing'Series

Distributors in U. K.

FOUNTAIN PRESS LTD.
65, Victoria Street, Windsor, Berkshire SL4 1EH
Telephone: Windsor 56959

1

Contents

The author would like to thank the following people and companies for their collaboration and support: Vicente Piera", for his judgement on materials and their use; Paco Vila Masip for his excellent photographic work; Eduard Tharrats of Fotocomposición Tharrats for his good work in spite of pressures; Salvador Gonzalez, Eduard José, Jordi Segú, Mercedes Ros; and all the staff of Instituto Parramón Ediciones, S.A.

Fig. 3.— A picture by the author, José M. Parramón, published in one of his books, ''Landscape in Oils'', as an example of painting *alla prima* (direct on to canvas without subsequent revision).

introduction

J.A. Dominique Ingres, famous French painter of the last century, offered his pupils this rule which is as simple as it is effective:

"You learn to draw by drawing"

It is good advice: nothing can teach as well as doing. I am wholly in favour of learning by doing, of dirtying your hands and doing it, and doing it again, of "drawing a hundred times the same stove in the studio", as Cézanne used to say to anyone who asked how to learn to draw. "Why then", I have sometimes asked myself, "write books that aim to teach drawing and painting?"

I have two answers to this question:

When I was fourteen or fifteen, and used to paint, I met a Majorcan painter named Forteza - who painted fabulous seascapes, small coves in Ibiza and Minorca with transparent blue sky and sea, full of light. One day I asked him, "Señor Forteza, how do you manage to get such a luminous blue?". He answered with another question: "Which blues do you use for painting?". I told him ultramarine and Prussian blue. "And cobalt blue? It's essential for creating luminosity!" That day I learnt that there was such a thing as cobalt blue.

A short time ago my friend Piera, the owner of a shop selling drawing and painting materials, talked to me about brushes made of man-made bristles:

"They are wonderful; they're the brushes of the future, cheap and with excellent properties. Not many know about them yet, but when they try them..."

Señor Forteza and my friend Piera, are like the paragraphs from one of my books. They explain, they give information, they show the difference between ultramarine and cobalt blue, between a brush of natural hair and one made of synthetic material. They indicate also, that there are brushes of sable and of squirrel.

Books can explain a process and they can explain it while "doing" it. In this book, for example, you will find a short history of oil painting, from the technical point of view. This helps to improve your knowledge of oil painting techniques in general. It is useful to know how Titian, Rubens, Rembrandt, Velázquez painted, and to know what each one of them contributed towards perfecting and varying basic techniques.

It is useful to know what a professional painter's studio is like, what his materials and tools are, and how they are used - all the materials and tools, from the traditional mahl stick, to liquid oil paint, sold in tins.

To be familiar with aspects such as cracking and the method "fat over lean", to read and know that "fat" means rich in oil, "Lean" is a paint greatly diluted with turpentine, harmonizing of colour and the ranges of colours, noting what is meant by, and what is the use of, tertiary or broken colours.

To do it, learn by doing, learn to paint by painting. With exercises explained step by step, illustrating by photographs the first, second, and the third stages, seeing how it is done.

In spite of everything, the pages of this book, and of all other books are not much use if you don't take your drawing block and draw, if you don't go out with easel and canvas and paint. I am with Ingres.

"You learn to paint by painting."

Well then, paint. I know of many who, thanks to one of these books, one day began and now paint. I also know of many who because they did not persevere, did not do it every day, ended by giving it up. You must feel the need to paint, not to leave it for tomorrow, to do it every day, today!

There is a story about Corot which tells how one day a friend went to see him to show him a picture. "It's good", said Corot, "but you'll have to redo and intensify this area". "You're right", answered the friend. "I'll do it tomorrow". Corot was alarmed and looked at him seriously: "What? Tomorrow? Not until tomorrow? And what if you die today?"

José M. Parramón

Fig. 4.— Corot. "Camino de Sevres". Louvre Museum. Paris.

Fig. 5.— Boticelli. "The Birth of Venus (fragment)"; Craft gallery. Florence.

history
of oil
painting

"The least essay written by
a painter will advance the
theory of the art better than
a million volumes".

Sir Joshua Reynolds (1723-92)

how they painted before the 15th century

Until Giotto there was no painting.
During the Middle Ages, from the 4th to the 13th century the art of painting stopped. The human figure was represented schematically, out of proportion, unrealistically, and influenced by religion. In the West, from the 6th to the 8th century, people moved from the cities to the country, kings had to leave too, fleeing the barbarians. "During this time", writes the historian Harnold Hauser, "nobody was capable of painting a human figure".
In the 11th century Romanic art appears. The paintings are still impersonal, religious, but in the late Romanic period there was already a freer and more individual form of expression. It was the prelude to Gothic art.
Starting from the 12th century, life returned to the city, and craftsmanship and trade gave rise to a new bourgeoisie. The artist belonged to a guild. He no longer worked always inside churches and under the direction of architect monks. Then he carried out the orders in his own workshop. He was the owner of his time and of the material he used. He could imagine and work on any theme.

In Italy, Giotto appears (1276-1337), an artist who painted real figures, real things, real scenes.
People painted in tempera *with egg yolk,* on wooden boards.
Up until the year 1410 artists painted in tempera. Tempera was used indiscriminately to paint miniatures, illustrations in manuscripts and missals, pictures, wooden boards, icons, decorative panels and walls.
Within the techniques of tempera painting, some artists had found that by applying linseed oil to a picture painted in tempera, the colours revived, and recovered their intensity and gloss. There were painters who experimented with mixing linseed oil with egg yolk.
The monk Theophile Rugierus wrote in the year 1200 a treatise on painting, *Diversarum Artium Schedula,* in which he recommended the use of linseed oil and Arabic gum.
It turned out that the oils and varnishes compounded from these formulas, dried very slowly making it necessary to expose a picture to the sun for days, with the risk of the painting deteriorating, the colours turning black, and the whites turning yellow.

Fig. 6.— Giotto. "Meeting at the golden gate". Scrovegni Chapel, Padua. Giotto, founder of modern painting, with Cimaube, painted with a realism, passion and imagination that had never before been seen, after the long night of the Middle Ages.

Fig. 7.— In the 15th century, the artist painted on a desk like the one that can be seen in this illustration, especially for painting medium size and small panels.

What is tempera paint with egg yolk?

The kind of colours used by the artists of the Middle Ages and the beginning of the Renaissance, were tempera colours, which were made up of pigments or colours in powder form, mixed together with a liquid made up of:

One fresh egg yolk
An equal part of distilled water

The technique of tempera painting is similar to that used for *gouache*. With tempera you can paint to give an opaque, all covering layer, or you can paint with transparent layers or glazes, depending on the extent to which you dilute the colours with the liquid.

Ignoring kinds of colours, any type of paint, just like tempera, is made up of colouring agents and a *medium or emulsion* which makes the pigments stick together. Thus, with a stick of wax colours, a tube of water colour paint, and a tube of oil paint, all three cobalt blue in hue, the colouring agent is always the same, *cobaltous oxide and alumina,* but the binding agent is different in each case, wax in the first case, water and a gum in the water colour, and drying oils and solvents in the oil paint. From this we can deduce that:

The medium decides
the kind of paint
The medium decides
the painting technique

Fig. 10.— Distilled water and a fresh egg yolk, are the ingredients needed to mix together the coloured pigments, in tempera paint.

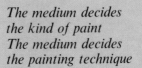

Fig. 11.— The coloured pigments, the basis of any type of colour, are supplied in glass jars or plastic bags. Of course they must be finely ground colours intended for artist's use.

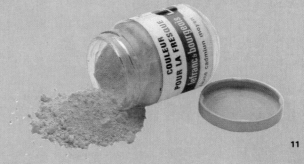

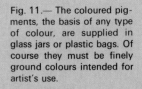

Fig. 8.— (Above). Medieval Art. "Christ in majesty (fragment)". Valltarga, Rosellón, France.
Fig. 9.— Duccio, "The Virgin with the Child and two angels (fragment)". Cathedral Museum. Siena. Duccio di Buoninsegna was one of the first artists of the Siena School of the end of the XIII century.

john van eyck's discovery

In the year 1410, in the city of Brujas, the capital of West Flanders, a young painter, named Juan van Eyck, put a picture painted in tempera and treated with oils, as recommended by the monk Theophile, to dry in the sun. Two days later, when he went to see how the drying was proceeding, he found to his disgust that the paint had cracked.

According to the story, from then on, Juan van Eyck did not rest until he had found an oil that would dry in the shade. It took him many months, after trying oils and resins of all kinds, he found that by mixing a small part of "white Bruges varnish" with linseed oil he obtained a mixture which allowed the pictures to dry in the shade with no trouble. (Some researchers have since confirmed that the "white Bruges varnish" was petroleum spirit or spirit of turpentine (turpentine), just like that we use today for thinning oil colours.)

Juan van Eyck then began to paint with white Bruges varnish and linseed oil, using them to mix the same pigments he used to paint in tempera, finding that the colours responded better, and that by increasing or decreasing the amount of varnish the colours would dry more quickly or more slowly. He found that he could apply *thin* layers (without linseed oil) or heavy ones (with more oil than varnish) and that while the colours were drying he could rectify or repaint without the previous colours being affected. The colours looked freshly painted and the picture would dry in the shade with no problems or risks. The "king" of painting had been born. Juan van Eyck had discovered the ideal painting medium.

The Flemish School

Juan van Eyck, who was then better known as "Juan de Bruges", had a brother, Hubert van Eyck, also a painter. The van Eyck brothers worked together in the same workshop, until September 1426, when the older brother Hubert died. His brother Juan finished the monumental picture "Ghent Altarpiece" in 1432, and from that date painted the pictures which have made the surname Van Eyck famous. Juan Van Eyck was an exceptional man and artist. When he was thirty years old he headed a movement rebelling against the prejudices and conventions of Gothic painting, defending and propagating the idea that "the men and women, the trees and the fields should be painted as they really are". Putting this philosophy into practice, Juan van Eyck convinced several artists of his time, among whom were the Master of Flemalle, the famous Van der Weyden, the young Petrus Christus... all Flemish, who from then onwards tried to paint with the realism and naturalness preached by Juan de Bruges.

The group created a school, the famous Flemish school, maintained and consolidated in the following years by Bouts, Van Goes, Memling, Jerónimo Bosch, Bruegel the elder, Rubens, Van Dyck, Jordaens, Rembrandt.

12

13

Fig. 12.— Juan van Eyck. "Eve from the Ghen Altarpiece". Temple of S. Bavón, Gante. The naked figure of Eve, with the realism and human quality Juan imparted to his work, attracted a lot of attention and became one of the symbols of the Flemish School.

Fig. 13.— In 1400, in Flanders, feminine fashion conditioned to a certain extent the shape of the female body, which presented narrow shoulders and full abdomen, as can be seen in the figure in the adjacent painting (fig. 14), here reproduced schematically.

Fig. 14.— Juan van Eyck. "Portrait of Giovanni Arnolfini and his wife". National Gallery. London. Here we have one of the best known pictures of the Flemish School of the 15th century. Observe the extraordinary quality of the detail, which today could be called, with reason, more than realistic. Note that this attention to details was achieved with successive layers of colour or glazes.

how the van eycks painted in oils

In 1437 in Florence, an old painter who was nearly eighty years old, was imprisoned for debt. His name was Cennino Cennini and thanks to the period he spent in prison, his name has become part of history as someone who understood and was a master of painting. While he was in prison he wrote a book, *The Book of Art*, which explains step by step all the processes and techniques, all the materials and styles that existed in painting in the 14th and 15th centuries. Therefore it seems that thanks to Cennino Cennini we can understand and reconstruct the way that Juan van Eyck and the artists of the Flemish School painted.

At the time there were already some artists who had experimented with painting on canvas, but the great majority, painted on thick wooden panels prepared with glue. Cennini said: "You should choose a panel of lime or willow without any defects. You should take glue made of parchment trimmings and boil it until three parts are reduced to one. You should test this glue with the palm of your hand and when you feel one palm sticking to the other, you will know that then the glue is satisfactory. And Cennini goes on with his literary instruction which summarized could be explained in this way: Onto the board they applied six layers of glue and several strips of old linen cloth. The board was put to dry and later they applied a layer of Volterra plaster and glue. Drying again and other layers of *Gesso Sottile*. At last it was cleaned with coal dust and pumice stone until the finish was white, hard and smooth as ivory.

On this board, the laborious preparation of which had taken several days, (the glue and the plaster was from two to five millimetres thick), Juan van Eyck and the artists of his time put into practice the following oil painting technique:

The construction of the picture was begun by first drawing with charcoal: "You should take willow charcoal and you should draw carefully. And you should go over the drawing with a fine pointed brush, soaked in

Fig. 15.— Juan van Eyck. "Santa Barbara". Royal Museum of Fine Arts, Amberes. This is the fine finish of a panel before beginning painting it in colours, as part of a laborious process of fine glazes. The picture reproduced above is about half the size of the original picture. Thus it is obvious that in the original panels, the artists of that time had to work in miniature.

Fig. 16.— Van Eyck's. "Virgin enthroned with child". Städelsches Kunstinstitut. Frankfurt.

the colour which in Florence in called *verdaccio*" (Cennini). *Verdaccio* was a mixture of black, white and ochre.

Once this drawing was finished the picture looked like the reproduction here, Santa Barbara by Van Eyck (fig. 15), which the artist left in this condition.

On top of this drawing they applied a fine layer of the same *verdaccio* colour, carefully working on the shadows, lights and reflections, until they had a perfect monochrome picture. In some cases, where the artist foresaw the later application of a bright colour (for example, clothing which in the end had to be bright red), he would leave this area with just the initial drawing, but without the later wash of verdaccio.

They began to paint with the clothing, continued with the architectural forms, the areas where there were landscapes, and so forth, leaving until the end the faces and flesh areas. This order followed the idea of having the whole canvas covered with colour when beginning to paint the faces, in this way managing to counteract the effect of simultaneous contrasts, which we are going to talk about in the following pages.

They painted with three tones for each colour

Fig. 17.— On top of the initial shadowing, carried out with *verdaccio*, the artist applied one or more layers of the local colour of the clothing.

Fig. 18.— With a relatively dark red, he applied the second tone, working on the shadowed parts.

Fig. 19.— Finally he applied a lighter red tone, mixed with white, to highlight the lights and the shining parts.

area, that is to say, for a red article of clothing, they prepared a red tone the same colour as the clothing (*local* colour), a second dark red tone for the shadows of the clothing (*dark tonal* colour) and a light red tone for the illuminated parts (*light tonal* colour).

Van Eyck and company painted with these colours in a way that is similar to how we now paint with water colours, that is by means of fine glazes (see on the next page a study on the technique of glazes), or thin layers of colour that were more or less transparent, according to the amount of oil and solvent, with the white of the background acting like the white of the paper in water colour painting.

They painted by areas. The artist painted for example, the Virgin's mantle; supposing this were red he began by painting a layer with the red tone of the local colour. This layer covered the white of the background, but allowed the shadowing of the original drawing to be seen through the local colour, and this, by darkening the red, provided a slight sense of volume (think how water colour works). On top of this first red layer Van Eyck painted with the second tone, dark red in colour, working on the shadows of the clothing, fusing and breaking down so that he could model the volume given by the folds and wrinkles in the clothing. Lastly, with the light red tone he highlighted the lights and shining parts of the clothing.

Once this first general scheme of colour was finished, they painted the faces and flesh of the figures. These still presented the patina of the first layer of verdaccio-remember? On top of this patina, they painted with the three corresponding tones of flesh colour —in transparent layers, obviously— so that here the flesh colour (light pink, or medium pink, etc) of the glaze played its part, and being transparent mixing into it the verdaccio colour, produced a drab-green colour which only needed pink and reddish tonings to supply the shades of flesh colour.

The work, finished with care and patience and final reliefs and emphasis, was produced with layers of light colours, sometimes even white, and as well some of dark brown and black.

The picture was left to dry for several days and was varnished.

the technique of glazes

The technique of glazes

A glaze is a transparent layer of oil paint, applied with the brush, on an area of the painting, in order to add a colour or to modify a colour that has already been applied. The glaze is made up of oil paint diluted with linseed oil and turpentine. The resulting mixture must be liquid, not thick. The technique of applying a glaze is similar to water colour technique. Basically it consists of applying successive layers of colour until you achieve the desired tone.

There is however an important difference. While a good water colour painter tries to obtain the colour with only a single layer, the oil painter using glazes, has to obtain the colour by means of several layers one on top of the other, to obtain the desired transparency, with the luminosity and richness of colour that is typical of layers painted in oil.

In order to achieve a luminous glaze the background must be light. A brilliant red dress, painted in glazes, must be painted on white or a light background. The glaze may be applied when wet, in which case the colour of the most recent layer mixes with that of the previous one losing effectiveness. Or it may be painted on top of dry or semi-dry, thus obtaining, by superimposition, all the qualities and effects of the glaze.

In any case, a lean glaze should never be painted on top of a fat glaze, that is to say, a glaze with a lot of turpentine and not much oil (lean), on top of a layer with a lot of oil and not much turpentine (fat), as the upper layer may crack. (We will talk about fat over lean later on).

Fig. 20 and 21.— Mantegna. "Virgin with Child". Staatliche Museum, Berlin. On the right a reproduction of Mantegna's unfinished picture (fig. 21), in a state somewhat more advanced than the "Santa Barbara" of the previous page 16. It must be noted that Mantegna painted here on canvas, and we can see its texture in the reproduction. Note the extraordinary quality of the drawing wash in *verdaccio*. In the above figure 20, I myself have begun the process of layerson the Virgin's face and neck, proving that it was a difficult, although very skilled job, but that it was extraordinarily slow. This skill —and I confess that I don't possess it, as it has to be acquired with practice—, allowed fantastic results, to be obtained with the appearance of lacquer or enamel, which in its time, must have been much admired.

21

how leonardo da vinci painted

Juan van Eyck died in 1441.

Years later, a painter of the Flemish School, Justus de Gante, who was a teacher in Ambers and in Ghent, left for Rome where his example meant that the Flemish techniques of oil painting were put into practice by artists in Rome and Florence, among whom was Leonardo da Vinci.

As you know, Leonardo da Vinci, as well as being a painter, was a sculptor, engineer, doctor, inventor... so it is not strange that all his life he was testing and experimenting with formulas for preparing surfaces, not to mention oils, resins and varnishes. Some of these experiments turned out to be expensive. For example, in the case of "The Last Supper", which he painted in oil on a plaster wall, the paint began to deteriorate before the painter died.

But Leonardo da Vinci was one of the greatest and most versatile men of the Renaissance, considered, together with Michelangelo and Raphael, as one of the three creators of the High Renaissance of the XVI century. His way of painting was completely personal. He dominated the *sfumato* and chiaroscuro techniques like no other artist, achieving volume in shadow and penumbra, painting the most gentle transitions in the tones from light to shadow...

Of course, Leonardo da Vinci knew Van Eyck's oil painting techniques, and fortunately he left us the testament of two of his pictures that illustrate this knowledge.

We can see them reproduced on the following page: above, left (fig. 25), the picture *San Jeronimo,* the figure of the saint in front of a lion, with a background of rocks and a building —on the right— in this kind of window formed by the rock formation. It is an unfinished picture, with which Leonardo da Vinci, in accordance with the Van Eycks' technique, followed the following process: First he drew the subject, with all elements of the picture, painting with dark *verdaccio* Secondly, he painted the figure of San Jeronimo in the same *verdaccio* colour, diluted with oil and turpentine. See how in the illustration this figure seems to have been painted in water colours. Note that he didn't paint anything else in this monochrome water colour technique. The lion, for example, is in the first stage of lineal drawing. Thirdly, Leonardo da Vinci painted, in a very dark brown, the rocky background, Saint Jeronimo's seat and the ground, using several

Fig. 22.— Leonardo da Vinci. "Self portrait" in compound charcoal pencil.

Fig. 23.— Leonardo da Vinci. "Mona Lisa (fragment)" Louvre Museum. Paris.

Fig. 24.— Leonardo da Vinci.— "Leda and the swan (fragment)". Borghese Gallery.

glazes. Lastly, he applied a few layers of colour to the left upper background, painting the sky, outlining some rocks and marking out what would probably be a sea horizon. And he stopped there.

Now look, below *San Jeronimo,* at the picture *Saint Anna, the Virgin, the Child and Saint John,* in a more advanced phase than *San Jeronimo.* Observe how in this picture Leonardo had used the following process. First, on the panel prepared in *gesso,* completely smooth and white, he drew the subject, first with charcoal and then with a brush and light brown oil paint (similar to verdaccio); Secondly, he painted the four figures with the same colour, diluted with turpentine and oil, applying several glazes, until he achieved a kind of monochrome water colour, thereby reaching the same stage as in the figure of *San Jeronimo.* At this point, following the ordered technique of the Van Eycks, Leonardo should have painted the construction or landscape that appears in the background of the picture, as he did in *San Jeronimo.* But it is understandable that he should dispense with the order followed by the Flemish painters and paint according to his own inspiration. Thus, Leonardo began to finish the four figures, giving us the opportunity to see what the old time painters really did, after the stage at which Van Eyck left *Saint Barbara* on page 16. The answer is here in this picture by Leonardo and even more so in the enlarged reproduction of the Virgin's head (fig. 27), where we can see on the one hand the effects of shadow accentuated by this greenish grey colour (was this then really the *verdaccio* colour mentioned by Cennini?), and on the other the effects of light painted with white, creating as whole a tonal composition of extraordinary quality, on top of which Leonardo —and like him the artists of the time— began, with the corresponding colours, the series of glazes which would complete the colouring, the volume and the contrast of the picture.

Fig. 26 and 27.— Leonardo da Vinci. "Saint Anna, the Virgin, the Child and Saint John". The original measurements of this work, exhibited in the National Gallery of London, are 159×101 cm., that is to say, more than a metre and a half high by one metre wide. Seeing it hanging in the museum, gives understanding what Leonardo da Vinci into did, how he constructed, how he began the colouring, how he studied the values, the light and shadow effects, and it represents a masterly lesson from the great artist of the Renaissance. If you go to London I recommend going to see this picture.

Fig. 25.— (Above). Leonardo da Vinci "San Jeronimo". Vatican Pinacoteca.

how michelangelo painted

Almost everyone knows Vasari.
Giorgio Vasari, born in Arezzo in 1511, painter, sculptor and architect.
But rather than for his works of art, Vasari is known for a book he published in 1550 when he was thirty nine, titled: *Le Vite de piu eccellenti Architetti, Pittori et Scultori Italiani,* an excellent and well documented account of the life and works of artists, from the Italians of ancient Rome, up to Michelangelo.
Vasari was a passionate admirer of Michelangelo Buonarroti to such an extent that he finished his book with a biography of Michelangelo, which was the first and only story of the life of an artist who was still living... "a faithful reflection of the greatest of the sculptors, painters, and architects who have ever lived".
Because undoubtedly Michelangelo was an exceptional artist, let us remember only the "Capilla Sixtina" in painting, the Dome of San Pedro, in architecture and the *Pieta* of Saint Peter or *Moses,* in sculpture, to agree that Michelangelo was really a genius.
Michelangelo Buonarotti's life written by Vasari tells us that the master gave great importance to techniques and processes for painting. For example, before beginning the frescoes of the Capilla Sixtina, he recognized that he did not know about the technique of al fresco painting and asked some fresco painters for help, and from them he learnt the job... although later he sent them packing, saying that they were no use at all. (Buonarroti, had a very bad temper).
Concerning his oil paintings, all on panels, Michelangelo began several and finished very few. One of the latter, which in itself qualifies him as an extraordinary painter, is *La Sagrada Familia/The Holy Family* (fig. 32), and we can deduce its technique of execution from two unfinished pictures Madonna and Child with the Infant Baptist and Angels (fig. 33) and The Entombment (fig. 34). The unfinished condition of these two paintings allows us to reconstruct, in effect, the techniques developed by Michelangelo in the painting of pictures in oil.
In the first place our attention is drawn to this kind of disorder or lack of method, half painting, for example, the two angels on the right, while the Virgin's face is almost finished although not completely—, and the two angels on the left haven't been finished yet. In the The Entombment the surprising

29

30

Fig. 28.— Michelangelo. "The Creation of man". Capilla Sixtina. Vatican. Rome.

Fig. 29.— Michelangelo. "The Dome of the Vatican". Rome.

Fig. 30.— Michelangelo. "Nicodemus self portrait". Santa Maria del Fiore. Florence.

Fig. 31.— Michelangelo. "Moses". Vatican. Rome.

thing is that the clothing is all in different stages of execution, with one of the figures (the one kneeling on the right, probably the Mother of God) not even started.

The same can be said of the flesh. The face and body of Jesus Christ shows the monochrome wash of the primitive construction. Saint John (dressed in red) already has the first glazes of colour, and Joseph of Arimatheaa's head, which appears behind Jesus, is so much more advanced in colour that it seems to be almost finished. It seems to me natural that Michelangelo should paint in this way but it demonstrates that he did not faithfully follow the rules of the Flemish painters who, in an orderly way, first painted the clothing, then the buildings and so forth and lastly the flesh. A further reference to the Flemish techniques, we can see, in the picture Madonna and Child with the Infant Baptist and Angels, that Michelangelo painted the faces, arms and legs of the two angels on the left in *verdaccio* leaving the clothing in white, a technique which, in principle, corresponds to that of the Van Eycks.

Perhaps the most interesting teaching point of this picture is in the Virgin's clothes which are brown, and almost black in the shadows and white in the illuminated parts. A white, which —it should be noted— you would guess not to have been painted on top of the black, nor by having left the plaster unpainted, but rather achieved by scraping with a scalpel. What colour could be reserved for the Virgin's clothing? I imagine that it was ultramarine blue, applied in glazes and therefore providing different tones, the same colour as that of the Virgin's mantle in the Holy Family (fig. 32). Now look at the two figures in The Entombment whose clothing Michelangelo painted with the same dark, brown colour as the Madonna and Child (fig. 34). In the two pictures Michelangelo's idea was the same. When he wanted to paint with a luminous colour, he painted the clothing with this almost black brown and then "opened" the white parts and applied later an intense and fairly uniform glaze which by transparency gave him the volume shown by folds and creases.

Fig. 32.— Michelangelo. "The Holy Family". Galeria de los Oficios. Florence.

Fig. 33.— Michelangelo. "Madonna and Child with the Infant Baptist and Angels". National Gallery. London.

33

michelangelo and raphael

Here we pause to comment on the assumption that Raphael painted with the same, or very similar, techniques to those of Michelangelo. In fact, when Michelangelo painted the picture *The Holy Family* (fig. 32), Raphael was barely twenty one. At this age he painted the famous picture *The betrothal of the Virgin* (fig. 36). Five years later he was called by Pope Julius II and soon he was the first master to be employed in the Vatican, with the single exception of Michelangelo who was working then in the Capilla Sixtina. Raphael then began one of his most famous works. *Las Stanzas.* He was twenty six and was considered a front rank painter, a genius comparable only to Leonardo da Vinci and Michelangelo.

When he was twenty, Raphael left Urbino where he was born, and moved to Florence. We know that here he worked very hard to learn all the processes and techniques of the Florentines. Five years later he was in Rome and associated with the best artists of the time, including Michelangelo. All these facts help us to confirm that Raphael —and the other artists of the time— painted with the same techniques as the master Michelangelo, who in his turn, had followed the steps of the Flemish artists.

34

ARTISTS WHO WERE CONTEMPORARIES of Leonardo da Vinci, Michelangelo and Raphael.

In 1510 Leonardo da Vinci was fifty eight years old, Michelangelo thirty five and Raphael twenty seven. As shown in this graph, in this same year of 1510, Bellini, El Perugino, Durero, Cranach, Jacob Palma, Titian (twenty three years old) were living and painting with great success. Raphael died young, at thirty seven, in 1520, and one year before, Leonardo died (at sixty seven). But Michalengelo who was eighty nine when he died, shared his fame with artists such as Titian, Bronzino, Tintoretto, Verones, Bruegel and even El Greco, who was twenty three when Michelangelo died.

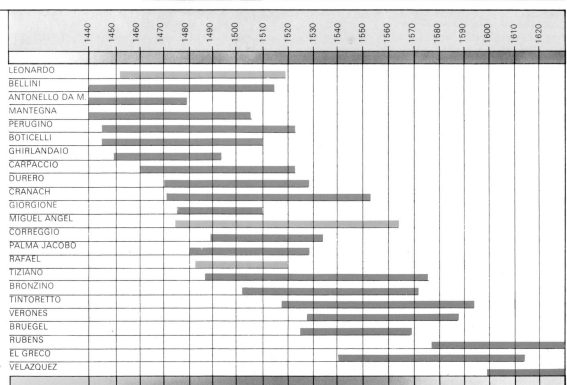

	1440	1450	1460	1470	1480	1490	1500	1510	1520	1530	1540	1550	1560	1570	1580	1590	1600	1610	1620
LEONARDO																			
BELLINI																			
ANTONELLO DA M.																			
MANTEGNA																			
PERUGINO																			
BOTICELLI																			
GHIRLANDAIO																			
CARPACCIO																			
DURERO																			
CRANACH																			
GIORGIONE																			
MIGUEL ANGEL																			
CORREGGIO																			
PALMA JACOBO																			
RAFAEL																			
TIZIANO																			
BRONZINO																			
TINTORETTO																			
VERONES																			
BRUEGEL																			
RUBENS																			
EL GRECO																			
VELAZQUEZ																			

35

36

Fig. 34.— (On the left). Michelangelo. "The Entombment". National Gallery. London.

Fig. 36.— Raphael. "The Betrothal of the Virgin". Pinoteca, Brera.

37

Fig. 37.— Raphael. "Virgin of the great Duke". Galeria Pitti. Florence.

titian, founder of modern painting

A few years after Juan van Eyck died, his successor as head of the Flemish School, Petrus Christus, was visited by Antonello da Messina a young Italian painter, who is said to have spent some time in Bruges, learning and practising the new technique of oil painting. Antonello da Messina went back to Venice and in a short time the Venetians had learnt the techniques of the Van Eycks. Among them was Giovanni Bellini, who as time passed, became the most important master of his generation. Amongst others, Giorgione, Jacob Palma and Titian were his students. He learned the secrets of the Van Eycks, and then adapted them to his personal way of seeing and doing things, creating a new way to paint in oils, considered to be the basis of modern painting.

The year 1550 passed. The Renaissance was reaching its end to give way to mannerism, an art of recherché themes, of complicated composition, of stylized forms (El Greco). For several years it had been more and more common for artists to receive commission for large pictures to decorate the walls and salons of the palaces of the time. In 1566, the Benedictines of Venice commissioned Paolo Caliari "El Veronés" to paint the picture *Las bodas de Caná* on canvas. Its dimensions are 6.66 × 9.90 metres. For this large size a picture on a wooden panel was not profitable, and hardly practicable. Canvas for painting was acquiring more and more adherents. The desk or sloping table on which small and large panels were painted, was changed for the workshop easel. Titian had been painting on canvas for some years already.

At this point in this short history of oil painting we must distinguish between "before Titian" and "after Titian". It was in fact Titian who revolutionionized the way of painting.

"Before Titian" artists painted in vivid, crude, exciting colours, as if instead of painting pictures, they were colouring stained glass windows. "After Titian", the colours were less vivid. They contained grey or blue or brown and were applied to the canvas to form a quietly harmonious whole.

"Before Titian" the painter always worked with brushes with sharpened points, and took pleasure in capturing details, endless minute details of jewels, curls, pearls and eyelashes, as if the merit of the work lay just in each of

Fig. 38.— Antonello da Messina. "Self portrait". National Gallery. London.

Fig. 39.— Titian "Self portrait". Museum of the Prado. Madrid.

Fig. 40.— El Veronés. "Las bodas de Caná". Museum of the Louvre. Paris.

Fig. 41.— Titian. "Danae receiving the rain of gold". Museum of the Prado. Madrid.

these details. "After Titian" they painted with bristle brushes, and ignored the detail in favour of the theme as a whole.

Titian was the first who saw and painted with the "optical grey" with which transitions from light to shadow acquire incomparable transparency and modelling.

Titian was the first who painted with a range of "broken" colours, the mixture of complementary colours and white in unequal proportions. (In later pages we will talk about this special range.)

Titian painted with brushed and also, in the last phases of the picture, with his fingers, something that other painters had already been doing, but not with Titian's perserverance.

He painted on coarse hemp canvas.
Instead of drawing with the attention to details of the Flemish School —remember *Saint Barbara* from page 16, figure 15—, Titian sketched the construction with no more than a few lines and immediately began to paint. This procedure gave rise to comments of all kinds from the artists of the time, such as Michelangelo's ironical phrase, quoted by Vasari "It's a pity that in Venice they don't start off by learning to draw properly". For his part Titian had said: "I don't want to construct too much. It disturbs my fantasy and doesn't let me paint."

Fig. 44.— Titian. "Christ crowned with thorns". Pinoteca, Munich. An example of the use of broken or "dirty" colours as Titian called them.

44

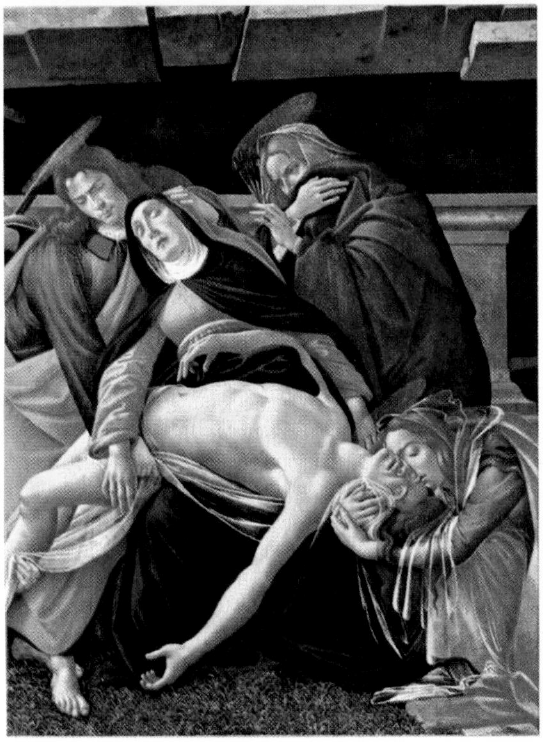

"Dirty your colours"

Titian was the first painter to discover the value of the dull, broken colours, and he applied them to his pictures, rejecting "the beautiful colouring" of the Flemish School. But the phrase Titian gave his followers, "dirty your colours", should not be interpreted literally, but rather with the idea of eliminating stridencies and achieving harmonies of more realistic colours, taking into account the fact that in real life colours are not pure, they are not clean like those in a stained glass window. In these colour mixture you can see an example of what we understand by "dirty colours":

42

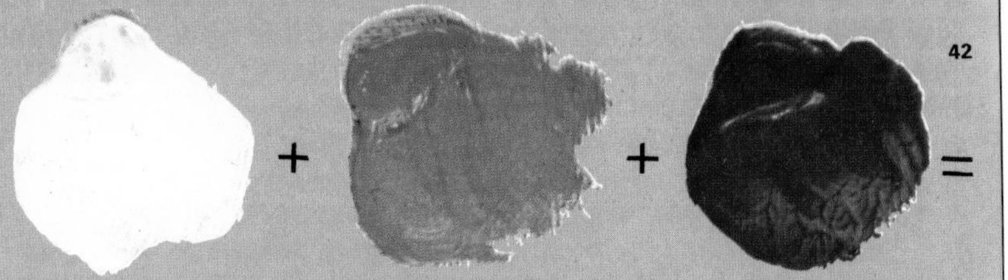

Mixing white

with a little ochre

and a little English red.

43

We get an excessively luminous flesh colour

but adding a touch of Ultramarine blue.

The previous colour becomes dulled giving a more realistic flesh shade.

Fig. 45.— Boticelli. "Pity", Pinoteca, Munich. Like all the artists who followed the style of the Flemish School, Boticelli painted with clear, clean colours in a way that was more decorative and less real than the way in which Titian's followers painted.

45

a revolutionary technique

Once he was ready to paint, seeing how Titian began the picture must have been a fascinating spectacle. Jacob Palma, Titian's young pupil describes it like this: "He spread over the canvas a layer of a certain colour which served as a basis for what he wanted to express. I myself have seen this intense background, all the same, painted only with *terra rosse* (red earth, probably Venetian red). Afterwards, with the same brush loaded first with red paint, then with black paint and subsequently, yellow paint, he painted the dark, medium and light parts and in four brush-strokes he had achieved extraordinarily well done figures."

Fantastic! Do you realize? Titian painted with half impasto using dense, covering paint, with the vision and spontaneity of an artist of today.

Titian called this initial sketch, painted in half inpasto, with a hog's hair brush, "the base of the painting".

After this first stage it was Titian's habit to place the picture face to the wall and leave it for weeks, even months... "until one day he took it up again" —Jacobo Palma goes on explaining—, "and looked at it critically, as if it were a mortal enemy... If he found something that he didn't like he set to work like a surgeon. Thus, by means of repeated revisions, he perfected his pictures, and while one was drying he began to work on another".

In the following phase Titian completed the model by means of a series of glazes —"Svelature? thirty or forty!" Titian used to say when people asked him if they were many or a few—, with which he returned to the classical method, but with certain variations. On top of the former "base of the painting", the artist applied glazes of bright colours in the illuminated parts and the same glazes, but more liquid, in the medium lights. The darker parts were not treated with glazes, they were left as they were. The bright colours of the glazes in each case were similar to the underlying colour. Thus, on red clothing, the glaze was a pink colour, and on flesh, it was ochre-yellow, and so forth.

The effect of these bright glazes on a dark background is comparable to a drawing done on a black slate with chalk rubbed in with the fingers, so that the dark colour of the slate is visible through the bright colour of the chalk... which promotes a series of grey gradations that later, when local colours are applied, will go on making them transparent, forming the classical "optical greys".

On this kind of monochrome painting some parts of which were already definitive, Titian applied series of glazes, painting, highlighting and accentuating.

The picture finished with sessions of direct painting, with half impasto and full impasto painting on top of the lights and bright parts, rubbing with the brush, which was called "frottage".

Titian, master of the frottage technique

46

The word frottage derives from the French verb frotter (to rub), and is used today in painting with a technique which basically consists of lightly loading the brush with thick paint, and rubbing on top of a part or area already painted and dry. The frottage or rubbing is generally applied by painting bright colours on dark ones, to complete steps from light to dark, shining parts, highlights and mid-tones. In figure 47 we can see the three phases of the frottage: first the area to be treated, a dark green spherical form on a dark crimson background.

Second, the brush loaded with greenish-yellow paint, scrubbing on top of the green colour, which is already dry, pressing from the outline into the inner part of the sphere, so that thirdly, the degradation is completed.

On the following page (fig. 48), in the portrait of Pietro Aretino, the technique of frottage was applied by Titian in a masterly way —for the first time— on the face, and very clearly on the yellow scrubbings in the reddish clothes of the model.

47

Fig. 47.— Background of priming colour used by Titian, on top of which he began what he called "the base of the painting".

Fig. 48.— (On the right): Titian. "Portrait of Pietro Aretino". Galeria Pitti, Florence.

rubens: half impasto and direct painting

Two hundred years after the Van Eycks, in 1650, as if he wanted to go back to sources, he painted with a technique that still has something to do with the Flemish painters. In fact; in the year 1650 the idea of abandoning the wooden panel and painting on a background —a previous priming— of brown or Venetian red, was already a common idea, followed by all the Italian artists. However Rubens went on painting on panels, except in large sizes, assuring the others that: "wood is the best support for small pictures", and on the other hand, Rubens did not accept the previous background with Venetian red and he applied, before beginning the picture, a layer of silver grey, to his panels and canvases. But his main contribution to the techniques of oil painting, was painting not only with glazes, but also with half impastos, that is, with covering layers, with colours that mixed on the canvas itself, painting directly, without waiting for drying periods, beginning and finishing a picture in a continuous session, as the painters of today do. This discovery of formulas and processes for painting faster, together with an extraordinary skill for drawing and painting, allowed him to become famous, painting pictures and portraits for all the nobles and kings of Europe. During his life he painted more than two thousand five hundred pictures, some of them of enormous dimensions like the series of twenty paintings on the *History of Maria de Médicis,* each one of which measures 4×3 metres.

Fig. 49.— Rubens. "Rubens and Isabel Brandt (fragment)". Painted a few months after marrying Isabel. Rubens was 37.

Fig. 50 and 52.— Rubens. "Elena Fourment". Historical museum of Vienna. (right hand page): detail.

In order to achieve this fabulous production of paintings, Rubens organized his work and his workshop, using his pupils and disciples, among whom was the portrait painter Van Dick, the animalist Snyders, Van Unden, Wildens who copied and extended projects, backgrounds, colour sketches, heads and bodies of secondary importance.

Stories tell us about Rubens "table-palette", a large, low table, with jars that held already prepared colours.

The workshop was large, with two floors. The second floor was in the form of a gallery encircling the room. On easels or wooden scaffolding for the large pictures, they worked on different pictures at the same time, and Rubens himself was there to initiate, rectify and construct...

Elena Fourment, Rubens' model and wife

Rubens married, for the first time, in 1609, Isabel Brandt. She died in 1626 and four years later Rubens married again, the very young girl, Elena Fourment. Elena was sixteen and Rubens fifty three. He had ten years to live, during which time Elena was the inspiring muse of all his pictures on mythological themes, as well as his favourite model for figure studies and portraits. When Rubens died, his widow wanted to destroy some of these studies like the one we reproduce on the following page (fig. 52). In this magnificent study the technique of glazes and half impasto is obvious in direct painting by Rubens. Observe the thin dark backgrounds, forms on top of dark areas (hair and ribbon or veil on the upper part of the head) defined with glazes: flesh, a first phase of wet glazes, and a second phase of half impastos (brighter flesh colours on the forehead, right side of the face, upper part of forearm, breasts, collar bones and so forth).

Fig. 51.— Rubens. "La Kermesse". Louvre Museum, Paris.

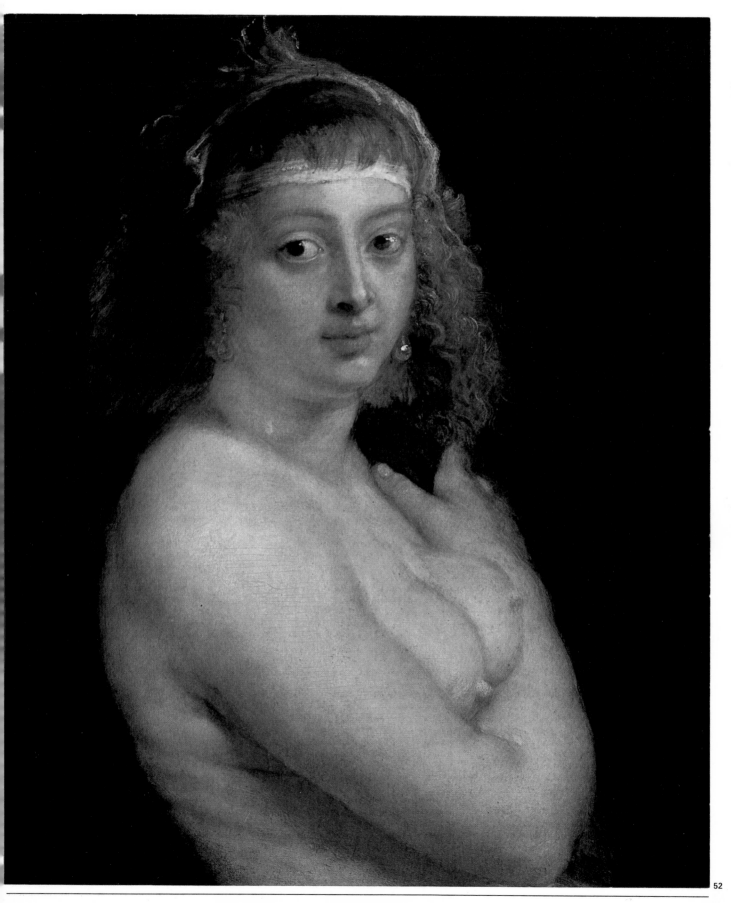

how rubens painted

Here we have Rubens' technique explained. On a wooden support, or canvas he first painted a layer of rather dark silver grey, on top of which he drew, and then painted, the theme of the picture in a brown wash. He went on accentuating lights and half tones, with glazes of light colours. Here Rubens recommended not "dirtying" the tenuous and transparent shadows with light glazes: "Paint the shadows carefully, but don't put white on top of them! It's poison for the picture!" And he further insisted: "If you paint with glazes on top of the transparent and golden qualities of your picture, your colours won't be luminous any more, but rather flat and grey."

Up to this point procedure was not very different from the one developed by Titian but from this phase on, Rubens painted in the shadows with glazes or half impastos that hardly covered anything. He painted with half and up to full impasto in the lights, especially the flesh, which he worked on with complete freedom, as Delacroix and Daumier would have done two hundred years later. See this head, on the right, a fragment of Rubens' picture *Saint Francis's last communion,* in which, in a graphic way, his techniques of half impasto and direct painting are demonstrated.

Fig. 53.— Rubens, "Saint Francis's last communion". Museum of Fine Arts, Amberes. One of his most important works, within religious themes, for its artistic composition —observe the play of forms and colours provoked by the canopy and the window or picture behind. As for the expressiveness of the figures, test this by looking at the enlarged head of Saint Francis on the following page, figure 55.

53

Rubens' technique

A) In the background, the upper and the lower left parts, we can see the thin layer of paint which hardly covers the grey priming of the panel.

B) On the head, above the ear, we can also see the thinness of the dark, almost black, layer.

C) The flesh colour —face, ear, neck—, was first stained with a glaze of clear ochre. This glaze can be distinguished in many parts of the face but specially on the ear.

D) Then there is a general modelling, slightly darkening some areas —on top of the eyelid, under the nose, and the left side, the chin.

E) He continued with a series of flesh coloured glazes. This work of glazes in superimposed layers can be clearly seen on the profile of the forehead, above the right eyebrow.

F) Rubens achieved bright impastos, with thick, opaque paint.

G) In the meantine he has clarified, with fine sable brush-strokes, the eyes, eyebrows, moustache and beard, and finally he accentuates the lights and shadows, painting the shining parts and details like the tear, the highlights of the eye, the red touch in the same eye —a true impressionist detail—.

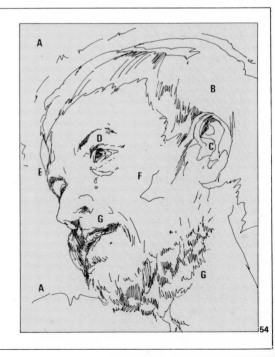

54

rembrandt: chiaroscuros and full impastos

Rembrandt was a self-taught man.
He never left Holland and yet, he learnt the *chiaroscuro* from Leonardo da Vinci, and from Titian he learnt to capture the lights and shining parts with thick, opaque, paint. "Why go to Italy?" he answered a question from a friend. "Why go to see them on their own ground if here in the Low Countries we have their pictures and can study them all the time?". To those who got very near the canvas to look at his pictures, and were astonished to see the "careless" finish and the thickness of the paint, Rembrandt said that the pictures weren't for smelling, but for looking at. And, in this connection, the impasto on some faces was so thick, that in Amsterdam there was a popular joke that Rembrandt's portraits could be hung up by the nose.

Some say that, influenced by Caravaggio's *tenebrism,* Rembrandt felt inclined to compose his pictures with special light and shadow effects, called *chiaroscuro* effects. In this respect, most of Rembrandt's picture offer a type of composition where the centre of interest, the figure of the group that forms the theme, is illuminated by direct light, while the rest of the picture remains in part shadow with enough light however, to see the forms and bodies that are in the shade. See on this page and on the following, the two magnificient examples of this artistic conception. In the upper right picture (figure 57) *The Holy Family,* one of Rembrandt's most famous, with the light focusing interest on the Virgin and Child, on the one hand, and on the angels coming down from heaven, while, behind the Virgin, Saint Joseph is wrapped in a chiaroscuro effect. On the following page *The adulterous woman,* (fig. 59) is a masterly lesson in the art of chiaroscuro, focusing attention on the group made up by the woman —dressed in white to increase the effect—, near Jesus who stands out because of his height, and surrounded by priests. At the same time, as in the upper part of the same scene, the profane cult goes on, the material richness is highlighted by the flashiness of the altar, and the throne and clothing of the officiating priest.

Imagine now these dark parts in both pictures, defined with a thin layer of paint and think that in the illuminated parts Rembrandt painted with full impastos, that is, with thicknesses of paint which differ little

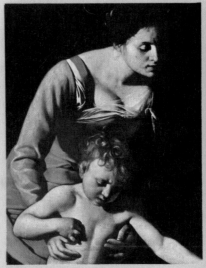 

56   **57**

Rembrandt's "chiaroscuro".

Fig. 56 anf 57.— (Left). Caravaggio, "The virgin of the the grooms". Borghese Gallery. (right) Rembrandt, "The Holy Family". Hermitage Museum, Leningrad.

When Rembrandt was 18 years old, it was only 14 years since Caravaggio had died. Caravaggio's style with its strong contrasts between light and shadow —the so called *Tenebrism*— prevailed and influenced all the themes and palettes of the time. But Rembrandt was already an artist with his own personality, who according to Sandrart repudiated most norms and rules from official Centres and Institutions. For him, intense light was not only the product of great contrasts, and on the other hand, intense colours did not help to create intense lights. The solution consisted in illuminating the colours, that is to say, in clarifying them proportionally to the light received. With these ideas and with a constant study of Nature, Rembrandt managed to dominate the art of the *chiaroscuro* like no other artist. This could be summarized as being *light in the shadow*.

58

Fig. 58.— Light scheme of Rembrandt's picture "The Holy Family". Here we can see Rembrandt's way of composing, to achieve the emphasis of the main point.

from those applied by some artists today. But let's leave this interesting theme for the next page.

Fig. 59.— Rembrandt. "The adulterous woman". National Gallery, London. Here we have a faithful reproduction of one of Rembrandt's most famous pictures, where the *chiaroscuro* effect and the meaning of this term is so obvious, that other explanations are hardly necessary. Chiaroscuro is the same as painting light in the shadow, as illuminating with tenuous colours and lights, the forms in the penumbra, so that they *are* in the picture. See these forms in this marvellous work by Rembrandt, and study the subjects that have been "abbreviated". See as Rembrandt knew how to see, the intense luminosity of the main subject, the adulterous woman kneeling before a God who is also a basic figure in this beautiful composition.

59

rembrandt, master of "frottage"

In 1642, Saskia died.

Saskia van Pilenborch had married Rembrandt eight years before, bringing him a good dowry and many friendships. Among these friends was captain Frans Banning Cocq, who placed a special order with Rembrandt to paint a large picture which would be the portrait of a group, 20 men, officers and soldiers of his company. The condition was that they should all look good, and some would pay more, others less, according to their position in the picture.

The picture measures 3.59 × 4.38 metres. *The Company of the captain Frans Banning Cocq,* very soon lost its long name to be called *The night round.*

Rembrandt fulfilled the order. The picture is one of the most famous of all Dutch paintings... but it was also the reason for disagreements and enmities because Rembrandt did not respect the positions selected for each person. Rembrandt had given up the idea of placing all the heads, face frontwards, and taking into account only his creative sense, he had arranged the models according to his own criteria, highlighting some heads and subduing others.

They say that because of this, Rembrandt did not receive more orders for a long time. His acquaintances withdrew their friendship and finally, almost ruined and alone, he shut himself in, physically and psychically. He ended up painting himself, painting a series of self-portraits, which have come into history as one of Rembrandts's whims. He painted a total of 60 self-portraits.

The self-portrait reproduced on the following page, the last-but one painted by the artist, when he was 63 years old, is a good example for studying Rembrandt's technique. Note that the background does not show any relief of paint while in the beret and the neck of the jacket, even though they are dark, the thickness and the brush-strokes are still visible. See, finally, that on top of a face colour of medium intensity but rather dark, Rembrandt applied thick paint, with not much on the brush, almost dry, following the *frottage* technique. By more or less scrubbing, using the brush, applying here almost pure white paint (shining parts of the nose and forehead, brush-stroke on the right eyelid, etc) there a light flesh colour tending to ochre, and dirtying in this or that area with a little sienna and blue (right cheek, near the ear). Painting with the technique of

6

scrubbing the brush which was loaded with thick paint, Rembrandt modelled the face creating superb solidity and colouring.

Don't think that Rembrandt always painted with the same technique, with an established formula. No, in this sense Rembrandt was an eclectic, a painter of endless resources and improvisations, who made use of any means available to achieve his goal. Hence, in the portrait of his mother (fig. 60), the lines which draw the embroidery on her underbodice were done by drawing with the tip of the paint brush handle. The paint on the forehead and nose is of an extraordinary thickness, while on the chin and jaw Rembrandt painted, engraved with the brush, rubbed, followed absolutely no rules at all. He was himself.

He was a real self taught man, Rembrandt.

Fig. 60.— Rembrandt "Rembrandt's mother". Van Bohlen Collection, Essen.

Fig. 61.— Rembrandt. "Self-portrait of the artist when elderly". National Gallery, London.

velázquez

"It's... as if he had invented oil painting all by himself."

This sentence is from the writer and art critic Raffaelli, and is quoted by Léon-Paul Fargue, who says, when talking of Velázquez: "He's modern, he foretells the future. There is a primitive (Van Eyck) in the portrait of the *Woman frying eggs* and there's a Courbet in *The Ladies in Waiting,* a Delacroix and a Degas in *The Spinners...*

Don Diego Rodríguez de Silva Velázquez, was born in Sevilla in 1599.

At the age of twelve he entered as a pupil in Francisco Pacheco's drawing and painting academy, in Sevilla. Pacheco was a painter and writer, and he wrote a book on the art of painting. *(The Art of Painting).* He had known El Greco, from whom he had first hand news about Titian's art, so that he was a good teacher for Velázquez. When he was eighteen years old, Velázquez was already one of the best painters in Spain. At this age he painted *The adoration of the Wise Kings,* the most important of his first pictures, in which, apart from the Caravaggian style, we have to stress the beautiful studied composition based on *The Golden Section,* formulated in the Renaissance (see a brief study on *The Golden Section* in the adjoining box). The Virgin painted in the *Adoration* is the daughter of professor Pacheco, and Velázquez married her the following year.

This and other pictures that Velázquez had already painted before the age of twenty —amongst others, the well-known ones. *Old woman frying eggs; The Immaculate Conception; The Water-carrier of Sevilla; Christ in the house of Martha and Mary.* These carried his fame to Madrid, and king Felipe IV, called him to paint a portrait. Velázquez was twenty three when he painted the king for the first time. Felipe IV was well pleased and named Velázquez painter of the royal house. Very soon Velázquez had his workshop and his house in the palace. This appointment gave Velázquez the chance to see and study daily and in depth the collection of paintings in the palace and among these were numerous important works of the Flemish School and by Titian, among others, as well as some pictures by Rubens and Rembrandt. For Velázquez the best and most important painter was Titian, who, at one time he said he liked even more than Raphael. Nevertheless when Velázquez was twenty eight, Rubens went to Madrid and made friends with

The law of the Golden Section

Fig. 62.— Velázquez "The adoration of the Wise Kings (detail)". Prado Museum, Madrid.

In ancient Rome in the times of Augustus, there was a famous architect, called Vitruvius, who established the "Law of the golden section". Which says:

"For a space divided into equal parts to be agreeable and aesthetic, between the smallest and largest parts there must be the same relationship as between this larger part and the whole space."

The arithmetic expression of the golden section is equal to 1.618. To find this ideal division, you only need to put the following formula into practice. Multiply the width of the canvas by the factor 0.618 and you will automatically obtain the division of the golden section. Lastly, repeating the operation for the height of the canvas, you will obtain a point which is considered ideal for placing the main element of the picture. The painter Velázquez, in his picture "The adoration of the Wise Kings", placed the head of the baby Jesus, right on the above mentioned point of the golden section. Velázquez's picture measures 200×125 cm. Multiplying 200 by 0,618 we get a number of about 123; and multiplying 123 by 0.618, we get 76. Where these two lines cross we find the point of the golden section. The same point may be right or left, above or below.

the Spanish painter, and they undoubtedly exchanged ideas about techniques and processes of oil painting. The year after he met Rubens, Velázquez made his first trip to Italy and in 1648 he travelled there for the second time. During this second stay in Rome, he painted the famous portrait of Pope Innocencio X and the only nude he painted in his whole life: *The Venus in the mirror.* Back in Spain he painted his most famous painting: *The Ladies in Waiting.*

Velázquez achieved his pictures by applying, basically Titian's techniques, as he was one of his admirers.

Fig. 64.— Velázquez. "The Ladies in Waiting". Prado Museum. This is considered to be the painter's most important work. The only work which allows us to learn what his physical appearance was like, as the figure of the artist looking at us with his palette in his hand, is really Velázquez. The Infanta Margarita surrounded by her ladies in waiting is the centre of the composition. The group of people in the foreground is looking at the King and at the Queen, whose images are reflected in the mirror in the background. We still don't know if Velázquez is painting the portrait of the king and queen, or if they are contemplating the infantas and their ladies.

64

velázquez

Velázquez discovered for himself, with the help of his master Pacheco and later with Ruben's confidences, the possibility of painting more directly —without so much glazing—, by means of half and full impastos. From this to painting with full impastos, mixing and composing the colours on the palette, taking them from the palette to the picture, like we do nowadays, there was only the passing of a few years during which Velázquez experimented alone, in his workshop in the Palace.

From the extensive information and documents that I have been able to gather together, I believe it's possible that Velázquez painted always on coarse canvas which he first covered with a uniform layer of *Venetian red,* exactly the same colour with which Titian sized his canvases before beginning the picture. Velázquez, like Titian, wasn't in favour of a previous drawing, in detail, like other famous painters of the time. He began the picture, like Titian, with the brush loaded with colour, painting and drawing at the same time. He worked over the whole picture, first, with a general half impasto, in the style of the base *of the painting* advocated by Titian. Velázquez did not plan or anticipate later highlighting with the traditional glazes and the typical three colours of the Flemish painters. For Velázquez this technique was out of date. He painted *directly,* but with a general first stage of colour where there was a predominance of grey —direct greys—, on top of which he then applied the definitive colours, which, in a spontaneous way maintained the primitive effect of the *grisaille* furthering the optical grey discovered by Titian.

On the other hand, Velázquez's way of making impastos, which contributes so much to seeing in the Spanish painter the workmanship of a modern painter, was the result of application of Titian's and Rembrandt's techniques, combined with those of Rubens. Note that Titian —Velázquez's model— was the first to paint with what I dare to call "thick glazes", or said in the painter's technical vocabulary, "frottage" (rubbing) and see that Titian applied these *frottages* with moderation. Observe too that Rembrandt made use of "frottage" a formula for creating volume, applying it decisively. Don't forget that both Titian and Rembrandt painted directly, as corresponds to the "frottage" technique. Meanwhile, Rubens, softe-

ned his way of doing it, inventing the *half impasto,* which, in the way that Rubens manipulated it, was nothing more than a series of "less thick glazes", paste-like, applied one on top of the other, mixing the shades on the canvas itself, some on top of others.

Velázquez knew how to see the advantages and disadvantages of both systems, and knew how to combine the two.

It was a process that was to some extent logical and was reached in Spain, at the same time as Velazquez developed it, by Poussin and de la Tour in France, Franz Hals and Vermeer in Holland, Reynolds and Gainsborough in England.

Fig. 65.— Velazquez "supposed self-portrait".

66

Fig. 66.— Velázquez. "Pope Innocencio X". Doria Gallery, Rome. The friendship between Rubens and Velázquez meant that the latter travelled to Rome, the first time in 1629, and for the second time in 1648. This second trip was really advantageous. He painted the magnificent and only nude of his life, "The Venus in the mirror", and he also painted the portrait of Pope Innocencio X, considered the best of all those he painted during his life. Before creating this famous portrait, he painted the one of his servant Pareja, showing his way of painting "in blotches" as people used to say or "with separate stains", or also in "his abbreviated way", meaning, as we now understand it "like an impressionist". Velázquez was daring enough to paint with this free, loose style the Pope himself. See and study on

the next page, the reproduction in black of the head of the said Pope, the relaxed but still certain workmanship of this incredible portrait.

Fig. 67.— Velázquez. "Head of the Infanta Margarita from the Ladies in Waiting". Prado, Madrid. This is how Velázquez painted, with this wide, sure brush-stroke —look at the eyes, the nostrils, the lips—, with this extraordinary synthesis more appropriate to a master of impressionism —see the way the hair is painted with these stains "which close up don't mean anything", representing flowers, or ornament, in the upper left hand part. Observe the texture of the canvas, the weight of the paint, the direction of the brush-stroke... What enviable facility!

velázquez best portrait

velázquez best portrait

from velázquez to picasso

Until the early 18th century, it cannot be said that there was any change worth taking into account. We can note, however, some variations: in the rococo period, for example when the painting of the Bouchers and the Fragonards offered a decorative and frivolous concept. The fashion was to paint with vegetable mediums, that is, instead of adding thick drying oils to the already mixed colours, turpentine was used, which meant that the colours dried quicker and produced a matt surface without gloss. This is a procedure which is valid today and which ensures that a picture will have a long life.

In the second half of the 18th century, the Neoclassical style made its appearance in Europe, and the colourbearer of this movement was the French painter Jacques Louis David. David and his school, in which we find among others, Gros and Ingres, during this period went back to Rubens' technique, of *transparent glazes combined with half impastos*. This technique the neoclassicists carried to its maximum height, reaching a perfection in the finish that was comparable to the paintings of Van Eyck and his followers.

The portraits of Ingres, which the philosopher Ortega y Gasset compared to the figures in a wax museum, are a good demonstration of the affectation of this technique.

With romanticism (up until the middle of the 19th century) this technique, then called *classic* continued, but there was the addition to the palette of the colours Bitumen of Judea and Mummy, two colours comparable to today's Cassel Earth, with the difference that they took a long time to dry. When the pictures were recently painted the colours appeared brilliant, with magnificent hues and contrast, but after a few years, they turned almost black, and deteriorated without any possibility of restoration.

Fortunately, there then appeared the luminous picture and the bright palette of the impressionists who reached their zenith between 1850 and 1870, with the pictures of Manet, Monet, Pissarro, Degás, Renoir, Sisley, Cézanne.

Fig. 69.— Boucher. "Woman resting". Pinacoteca, Munich. In the French rococo it was the fashion to paint with solvents, instead of oils. Rectified turpentine was one of them and it is still used today to achieve lean paint.

Fig. 70.— Ingres. "Self-portrait", Museum of Fine Arts, Amberes.

70

Fig. 71.— Ingres. "Portrait of Mlle Riviere". Louvre Museum, Paris.

Fig. 72.— Jacques-Louis David. "The consecration of Napoleon I". Louvre Museum, Paris.

69

71

72

oil painting today

Up until the last third of the 18th century, oil colours were made up by the artist himself or by his helpers, according to methods which we will study later. At the end of the 18th century, colours were already prepared and sold in small skin bladders. The performance of these colours was very uncertain, as the preparation was done in a very empirical way, without any guarantee that a certain colour —ultramarine blue for example— would always have the same hue, intensity and consistency. From 1850 to 1860 the first oil colours packaged in collapsible metal tubes appeared on the market. There was considerable trial and error as regards the quality of the paints, but finally the manufacturers achieved oil colours of a consistent quality. Also the new manufacturers offered a much wider range of colours, with a gloss and richness that the masters of ancient times could never have imagined. Renoir said, in his later years: "Tube colours allowed us to paint in the open air, from natural models." Without these colours in tubes neither Cezanne, nor Monet, nor Sisley, nor Pissarro would have existed, nor would there have been what journalists called "impressionism".

And to Picasso.
The quality of the materials and especially that of oil colours since the beginning of the present century, make any kind of support possible, from paper to a brick wall, from white sizes to black sizes, painting with a brush, with a knife, in squirts, just as the paint comes out of the tube, in layers so liquid or thin that the canvas is texture instead of just a support...
Anything can be done, and the material always responds, provided that a few basic rules are always respected, and we are going to talk about these throughout this book.

Fig. 73.— Turner. "Storm at sea", Tate Gallery, London. Turner already painted like an impressionist at the beginning of the last century. His technique was completely personal, and he often applied the technique of rubbing.

Fig. 74.— Cézanne. "Self portrait with a cap". Hermitage, Leningrad. Of almost actual size, this reproduction shows us the free, confident and completely spontaneous way in which Cézanne painted, in a style that goes beyond impressionism.

Fig. 75.— Van Gogh. "14th of July in Paris". Collection Jaggli Hahnloser, Winterthur. Already at the height of *fauvisme*, Van Gogh develops a technique of thick impastos with paint that is practically "coming out of the tube", and completes the picture in a minimum of time.

Fig. 76.— (Following page above) Vermeer. "The painter in his studio". Historical museum, Vienna.

the painter's studio

"You will have your workshop where nobody will disturb you, and which has a single window. Near this window you will place your desk as if you were going to write".

Cennino Cennini (1390)

the early history of the painter's studio

Have you ever asked yourself what the studios of the great maestros of the 16th and 17th centuries, Rubens, Rembrandt and Velazquez... were like?

Of course they all worked in large rooms, large areas which were in no way different from those occupied by other artisans, like the tailor, the carpenter, the boilermaker. The studio was the workroom.

Velazquez's workroom measured approximately six metres high by five wide and was about ten metres long. The painter Juan Bautista del Mazo, a disciple of Velázquez, painted a picture entitled *Velazquez's family*, and its scenary is the maestro's studio (fig. 79). We know, on the other hand, that the picture *The Spinners* (fig. 77), was painted by Velazquez in his own studio, although he modified the structure slightly, especially that recess in the background which he painted in a somewhat more stylized way. Lastly, the picture *Las Meninas* was also painted by Velázquez, in his own studio, placing the figures in the same place and with the same illumination as the spinners in the foreground and Velazquez's family.

In the studios of the time, there was, next to the large chamber, a rather small room, where there was running water and a stove, as well as a table or bench for grinding colours. In this room, as well as different tools, there were small bags of coloured pigments, bottles of oils, resins and solvents, and small containers holding colours that had already been made. These were all stored on shelves and in cupboards, the whole rather like a rudimentary kitchen, in which we must remember, the painter's apprentices "spent six years", according to Cennini, "grinding colours, cooking the glues and mixing the plasters". This kind of kitchen still existed in studios until no more than about fifty years ago, and hence, even now, when we see a painting or picture that has been very manipulated, with special textures or finished, we hear a comment something like "there's a lot of kitchen work here".

At the end of the last century the studio of famous painters became a small museum and reception salon. The painter's tools were an accessory and most important was the decoration, with old furniture, tapestries, copper vessels, oriental hangings and fabrics. In Paris, the painter Gerome rented a small palace in front of the Moulin-Rouge, in which there was a series of luxurious salons,

sculpture and painting workshops, full of objects of art and oriental curios. This was a real museum in which the artist used to hold receptions and at the same time sell his pictures. The *realists* first, and later the *impressionists,* with the coming at the same time of halls or galleries for exhibiting pictures individually, finished with the studio-museums in the style of Gerome, establishing a normal workshop-studio, even though we now consider the dimensions excessive. The two pictures reproduced on the following page illustrate something of this studio of the end of the last century and the beginning of the present one, allowing us to see and study the workshops of Courbet (above) and Bazille (below).

Fig. 77.— Velázquez. "The spinners". Museum of the Prado. Madrid.

Fig. 78.— Del Mazo, "Velazquez's family". Historical Museum. Vienna. The thematic value of this picture is not so much in seeing and meeting Velazquez's family, as in the group being situated in the painter's studio. See in the background, Velazquez himself painting, and observe the similarities of this room with the one in the picture "The spinners".

79

Fig. 79.— Courbet. "The painter's workshop". Museum of the Louvre. Paris. The picture shows us Courbet's studio in reality, when the artist still painted the practically naked walls. Courbet wanted to present in his workshop, his models, and people with whom he had worked within these four walls.

Fig. 80.— Bazille. "Bazille's workshop". Museum of the Louvre. Paris. Painter's studio, typical of the end of the last century, with piano, wide window, with black curtains for controlling the light, stove and attic with a room for spending the night (the stairs on the left confirm this, which was normal).

80

the painter's studio today

Fig. 81.— A corner of Pissarro's studio, with the artist painting. The type of easel is still made today and is common in Fine Arts Schools.

81

Fig. 82.— A view of part of Cézanne's studio in Aix en Provence, where we can see a type of easel suitable for large pictures. Strangely enough Cézanne had no pictures on the walls of his workshop.

82

Fig. 83.— Picasso. "The bath". A picture in which Picasso reproduced his own room, the room he had for a studio in Paris, in the *boulevard* of Clichy.

83

About 1890 Camille Pissarro and Paul Cézanne lived in the country, and had their studios in country houses. Ground floor, one or two normal windows, walls with pictures hanging... a normal room but still spacious as befitted the rooms of old country houses.

In 1901, Picasso travelled for the first time to Paris and stayed in a room on the boulevard Clichy that did not measure more than 4 × 5 metres. In this room Picasso lived and painted. He made it his studio. This is proved by the picture *The bath* in which Picasso reproduces his own room (fig. 83).

Picasso returned to Spain and went back to Paris in 1904. The sculptor Paco Durio, wrote to him a month before he set out, offering him the studio he had had in Paris up till then a room on one side of Montmartre, at number 13 *rue de Ravignan* (today Place Émile Goudeau). "Simple, cheap and in a beautiful quarter", Picasso's friend Paco Durio told him.

Picasso's new studio was an old ramshackle wooden building, which, as Picasso used to say laughing, when the wind and rain grew strong, "swayed like a yacht". Max Jacob, the poet, henceforth called it *bateau-lavoir*, remembering the old floating wooden laundries anchored in the Seine. The famous *bateaulavoir* must have been really large, bearing in mind that up to 15 people used to meet there. From what has been said we can deduce that the means —in this case— the dimensions and the location of the studio, do not have a decisive influence when it comes to creating and painting. However, there are minimum conditions regarding the place, the space, the light and the materials. We are beginning by specifying the minimum dimensions of the studio:

a minimum space of about 4 × 3.5 m is adequate but a larger room is preferable.

85

Figs. 84 and 85.— A painter's studio, in a high city flat, just as it might be nowadays, made up of one room (9×3.5 m.) half of which is used for painting, and the other half for reading, listening to music, and chatting with friends.

Fig. 86.— Here we have Francesc Serra's studio, in a garret in the old part of Barcelona —a building with seven floors—, with the artist himself painting. If is a room of 4×5 meters lit by three windows, as seen in the photograph, that is, by means of *cenital* light (from above).

Fig. 87.— Corner of my own studio in a country house. It measures 6×5 metres and has a large picture window 1.70 m from the floor (see figure 88 on page 52).

87

lighting of the studio

On another occasion, while I was in Francesc Serra's studio seeing how he painted a figure, I noted that the light came from a picture window placed about two metres from the floor, giving, a quality and direction that we could call *cenital-lateral*.

Then I remembered Velázquez and his studio with a large open picture window in the upper part of one of the side walls and I thought of the possibility of building a modern studio having this kind of natural illumination. This studio can be seen in reproduction (fig. 88), where I now work with very good results. The lighting is diffuse but gives pleasant contrast, for painting in general and especially for painting figures and portraits. The direction of the light, and the above mentioned diffuse quality, eliminate any reflection or shine. The sloping roof, of varnished wood (a warm colour), compensates for the intensity reflected from the white walls (cold tendency) balancing, as a whole, the colour of the light and the intensity.

Most painters work and paint by day with natural light. Which does not mean that if one wants to, one cannot paint with artificial light. There are many professionals who "carry" two paintings at a time, one in the morning, painting by daylight, and another in the evening or at night, painting by the light of one or more electric lamps.

Painting with natural light the studio should have at least one large window which allows one to paint by daylight, lighting the model in a frontal lateral or lateral direction. Painting by artificial light one needs two lamps, one to light the model and another to light the picture one is painting. Also it is a good idea to have an additional light for general illumination.

To illuminate the model, whether it is a figure or a still life, we only need a single 100 watt lamp set in a large white reflector in order to avoid the effect of focus or directed light and the excessive contrast it would produce. To paint a still life or a portrait the lamp should be placed at about a metre from the model.

The illumination of the picture should be projected from above with a swan neck lamp or extending arm set up on the workshop easel (see fig. 95 on page 55), with a 100 watt lamp as well. To avoid unbalances between the light on the model and that on the picture it is important to work with two lamps of the same power.

Fig. 88.— Cenital light, lighting from above, through picture windows situated 1.70 m from the floor.

Figs. 89, 90.— Artificial light can give rise to reflections (89), which can be eliminated by sloping the canvas and painting diagonally or vertically. (90)

Lastly, the auxillary light should be installed quite high, near the roof, with at least a 100 watt lamp (depending on the dimensions of the room).

89

Fig. 91.— Illumination with natural light coming from a wide window. In the photograph of the model we can see that the shadows pro-jected are soft, without any clear-cut edges. The colour of the light is neutral or with a tendency to blue.

Fig. 92.— Artificial light coming from a table lamp with 100 watt bulb. The contrast is accentuated, the shadows seem cut out, clearly defined and darker. With a tungsten lamp the colour tends towards yellow. This is not really important, as you only have to change it when painting or accentuate it deliberately.

Fig. 93.— I painted this sketch in the studio reproduced in figure 88, with cenital light, capable as you can see, of providing soft illumination similar to natural light. To accentuate the contrast, it's only necessary to pull the curtains, reducing the opening, and you have a more direct light.

contents and illumination of the studio

Fig. 94.— Here we have a painter's studio 3.5 m wide by 4 m long, drawn to scale, with the dimensions of the furniture in keeping with these measurements. Here there is everything needed to work comfortably, that is:

Illumination
1. Windows.
2. Table lamp.
3. Extending light on the easel.
4. Extra light for special effects.
5. General light (in the roof not shown in the drawing).

Furniture and tools:
A. Workshop easel
B. Small table or extra piece of furniture for painting.
C. Stool
D. Auxiliary rectangular table.
E. Bookshelves.
F. Musical equipment
G. Loudspeakers
H. Divan bed.
I. Auxiliary table, chair, armchair.

Here we have the drawing of a studio seen from above, showing the furniture and tools, and the number of sources of light and their positions. Note that apart from the equipment and tools for painting, there are items of furniture such as a divan bed, bookshelves with musical equipment and an extra table

DIMENSIONS

**4 metres long
3,5 metres wide**

taking these dimensions as minimums

which can be used both for placing a still life, and for writing, drawing, making sketches and plans. The distribution of the light sources is functional. The general light of the studio, hanging from the roof is not shown here.

furniture and tools

The furniture and tools that are essential for painting are limited to an easel, a seat and an auxiliary table for tubes of paint, cloths, bottles of oil and turpentine, a container for brushes. (see fig. 95).

As far as the easel is concerned, pages 58 and 59 show a number of variations of the basic so-called outdoor and workshop easels.

The auxiliary table, for painting, can be found in shops selling drawing and painting equipment where they sell furniture designed for the purpose. The piece of furniture shown in figure 96, has wheels which allow it to be moved around the studio.

As a substitute for this, you can use any normal table. Some time ago, I myself, adapted an old typewriter trolley for this job, putting a table on top and I finished it by adding a drawer at the bottom (fig. 97).

On the other hand I recommend buying a folder stand like that shown in figure 98, very desirable for storing drawing paper or finished work.

95

96

97

98

auxiliary furniture

Some people paint standing up, but generally speaking most artists paint "half sitting", that is to say, on a seat or stool that is higher than normal on which one can half sit down and can stand up with almost no effort. There are two typical models: the chair, with wheels —this is important— with a slightly flexible back, and a covered seat that you can raise or lower, and having a bar at the bottom to rest your feet on (fig. 99). Another type is a wooden stool with three legs, with an adjustable seat, as shown in figure 100.

The studio table has to provide a place to write, plan, and draw. I recommend a model like the one in figure 101, made up of two independent stacks of drawers and a sloping table top which is placed on top of the two stacks, without being fixed, so that you can separate the two as desired.

Fig. 99.— Chair with covered seat and back. The back is adjustable and flexible. The chair is on wheels and above them there is a rest for the feet. The height is adjustable and it is of all metal construction.

Fig. 100.— Typical wooden stool, with three legs and a seat that can be adjusted by means of a screw shaft. Both seats are higher than a normal chair, so that it is possible to work half standing, half sitting.

Fig. 101.— Studio table especially designed for drawing, planning, designing, and so forth. It is made up of two sets of four drawers each, and a sloping top.

The top, as you can see in figure 102, is independent of the sets of drawers, so that it is possible to separate the drawers to a greater or lesser extent to increase the lenght of the table as required.

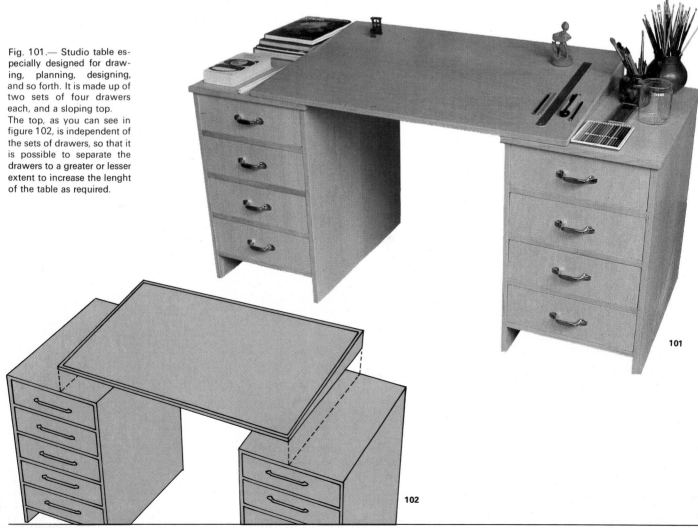

99

101

102

materials
and tools

the easel

There are two kinds of easel for oil painting: The outdoor easel for painting in the open air and the workshop easel for painting in the studio.

The outdoor easel is basically made up of a wooden tripod, designed to fold up for easy transportation. It must fulfil the following conditions: a) it must be light, rigid and high enough to paint standing up if desired. It must be adjustable for the height of the picture, and it must firmly support the picture at the top. A standard model of this easel see figure 103.

Among the outdoor easels, one of the most commonly used by the professional is the easel-box (figures 104 and 105) and its most

important characteristics can be summarized as follows:

Slope the picture as desired. Possibility of painting several different sizes from a number 1 landscape to a number 30 (92 × 65 cm), the facility for lowering or raising the whole thing by folding its legs and the possibility of leaving the drawer, which stores tubes and paints half open, thus providing a solid platform on which to rest the palette. Lastly, see in figures 106 to 109, several models of workshop easels, with the common feature of a tray with a rack which allows the picture to be lowered and raised as you wish. See in the texts of the following page, upper part, the features of these models.

Fig. 103.— Outdoor easel-tripod, for painting in the open air. Classical model brought up to date, with two supports to hold the palette while painting. It is shown also folded up.

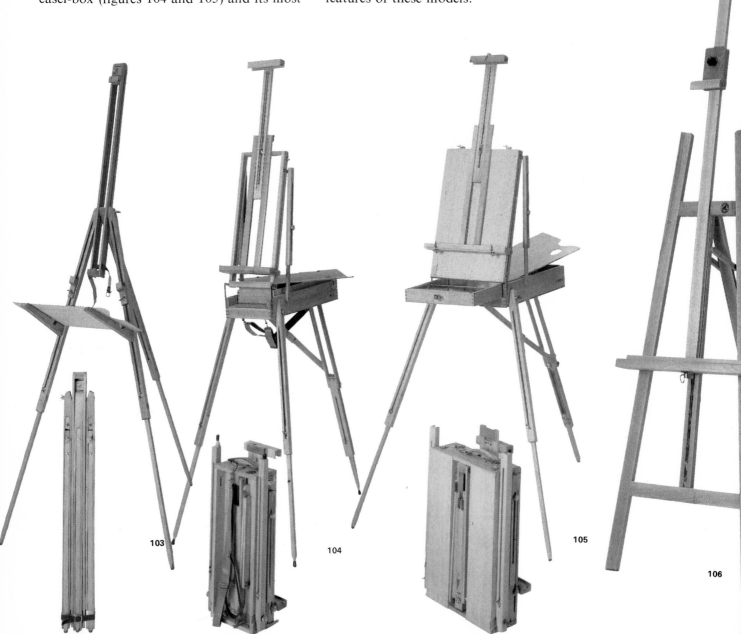

103

104

105

106

Fig. 104.— Outdoor easel-box. Latest model of easel-box, narrower, lighter and in general less troublesome than earlier types. It offers the same advantages as the classical model in figure 105.

Fig. 105.— Folding outdoor easel-box. It is the traditional model designed more than forty years ago, which enables it to be carried in one piece no bigger than small suitcase, along with all the tools materials necessary for painting, including the canvas if it is not very big, with brushes, tubes, solvents, knives, charcoal, rags, and so forth.

Fig. 106.— Classic workshop easel, used for centuries.

Fig. 107.— Workshop easel with similar features to the previous one.

Figs. 108 and 109.— Workshop easels, classical models, with wheels, solid and stable, allowing us to paint large canvases, with trays for temporarily leaving brushes, tubes of colour, knives, etc. The model in figure 108 offers an additional adjustment which allows the artist to slope the canvas forward in order to work more confortably and to eliminate reflections.

107

108

109

the palette

Signac, the first *pointilliste,* describes the work of his friend Seurat, also a pointillist, in this way... "He perceives the contrast, distinguishes the reflection, plays with the tin lid that he uses as a palette..."

Genevieve Laporte asks Picasso

—"But don't you use a palette?"

—"No", answers Picasso, "as you've seen my palette is a newspaper.

When the page is completely full, I pull it off and throw it away... sometimes it's a pity, as my palette has turned out like a good picture. Matisse has more opportunities. He uses a plate as his palette! What a pity! Picasso couldn't see them, nor use them but nowadays you can buy paper palettes in the shops! They came out a short time ago: just a block of papers, in the shape of a palette, which has the main advantage of being able to use a fresh palette whenever you like just by tearing off the page you have already used.

But, of course, a paper palette does not suit everybody, and the usual thing is to paint with a rectangular or oval wooden palette. The form has been a matter of individual taste for many years, If, out of curiosity you look at page 49, you will see that Courbet was already painting with a rectangular palette more than a hundred years ago, while Bazille at more or less the same time, had an oval-shaped palette hanging on the wall of his studio (right hand column). It's true that nowadays more rectangular palettes are sold than oval ones, but I dare say that this is not because of advantages or disadvantages of one or the other, but rather because it is much easier to manufacture rectangular than oval ones and therefore there are more rectangular ones.

Lastly, there are also plastic palettes, which are not to be looked down on if you remember that they can be cleaned easily. Personally I paint with a rectangular or oval palette, it's all the same to me, but it is always a wooden one.

Fig. 110, 111 and 112.—Common types of rectangular and oval palettes. The last one, a white one, is made of plastic. At present I believe that rectangular palettes are used more than oval ones, perhaps because all paint boxes include rectangular palettes and this circumstance favours the habit. In any case there is no difference from the technical point of view. It is rather a question of use and habit. The last of these palettes is made of plastic. At present I believe that rectangular palettes are has the advantage of being able to be cleaned in an instant, and well. Personally I use wooden palettes.

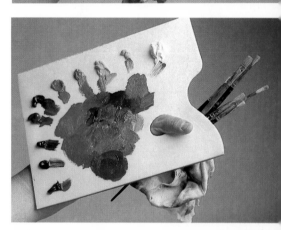

Fig. 113.— Dippers; containers for linseed oil and turpentine, used while painting, can be attached to the edge of the palette (see in fig. 10), by means of the spring clip seen in this illustration.

paint boxes

The paint-box for oil painting, forms a vital part of the artist's equipment, used for painting in the open air, country landscapes, urban landscapes, seascapes. The paint-box can also be used in the studio as an auxillary piece of equipment, while you are painting, to hold and leave brushes, tubes, cloths.

The most common and well known paint-box, is the same as the type shown in figure 115/116. Its special advantage is that you can carry the palette without cleaning it, that is with the remains of colours that are left at the end of a painting session and also, allows us, thanks to movable strips of wood with clips (A), to transport a number 5 canvas that has just been painted, without any risk of marks. The arrangement of these strips of wood and the calculated slope of the lid, allow us to paint without an easel. It is worth mentioning the models of paint-boxes shown in small scale in figures 114 and 115. The first of these (below) is made completely of plastic, so you can pack in tubes, dippers, bottles, even brushes.

Fig. 115.— Wooden paint box, smaller size, solidly constructed, very nice and functional.

Fig. 116.— Paint box, classical wooden model with metal compartments. It lets you carry everything you need for painting in the open air. The guide-strips inserted in the lid allow you to carry a number 5 canvas-covered cardboard, after painting it and while the paint is still damp, because it is separated from the palette and the bottom of the lid.

115

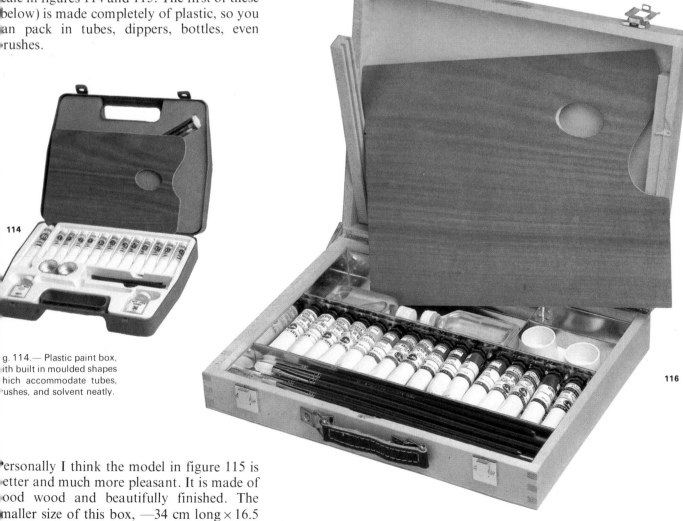

Fig. 114.— Plastic paint box, with built in moulded shapes which accommodate tubes, brushes, and solvent neatly.

114

116

Personally I think the model in figure 115 is better and much more pleasant. It is made of good wood and beautifully finished. The smaller size of this box, —34 cm long × 16.5 wide and 5 cm deep—, makes this model a really functional paint box.

canvases, cardbord, surfaces

The best canvases for painting in oils, are made of linen or cotton. There are still some who paint on hemp, but this is an exception. Linen canvas is undoubtedly the best and can be distinguished by its stiffness and somewhat dark greyish-ochre colour while cotton is softer to the touch and is light grey in colour. Some manufacturers dye the cotton so that it looks like linen.

Within these groups, the artist can choose between canvases with fine, medium or coarse weave, with more or less *priming. The priming* is a layer of rabbit or carpenter's glue, mixed with plaster (Spanish white) and zinc oxide, which prepares the canvas —the wood, the cardboard or any surface at all— for better adhesion and future perservation of the painting. The priming formula mentioned provides a white layer, but you only have to add a grey or Sienna coloured powder to get a coloured priming, as Rubens (grey), or Titian and Velázquez (Venetian red) used to do.

The priming of canvases or any other surface, may at present be done with acrylic paint, or with paint that has been especially prepared for this function ("priming white" from Winsor and Newton, for example).

The canvas can be bought, mounted on a stretcher, or in a piece, sold by the metre. Rolls of canvas measure from 0.70 to 2 metres in width. A stretcher is a wooden frame which has small wooden wedges in the corners which allow you to tighten or slacken the canvas.

The old wooden support today has become a thin sheet of plywood or pressed wood, that is flat, light and rigid. A sheet of wood can be prepared with a layer of thin carpenter's glue. To paint sketches, notes and small sized pictures it is common to use prepared cardboard with a smooth, white, matt primed surface. In the same way as wood, cardboard can be prepared by the artist, priming both sides to avoid deformations caused by moisture.

There is also canvas-covered cardboard, which does not need any preparation at all.

Lastly it is worth remembering that for plans and small sketches high quality drawing paper (Canson, Caballo, Scholler, etc.) serves perfectly well.

PRIMING SURFACES FOR PAINTING

Taking into account the fact that in shops selling drawing and painting materials there is a wide assortment of canvases with stretchers, sheets of cardboard, and wood, perfectly prepared, of all sizes and kinds, of medium and high quality, to a certain extent it seems absurd to want to prepare the canvas oneself, to make the stretcher and to put it together, wasting precious time and running unnecessary risks. So that it cannot be said we have ignored this point and in case you have to do it one day, here is a priming formula and instructions for using it:

The sizing
Ingredients:
70 grams of carpenter's glue (Cologne or rabbit glue) and a litre of water.
Leave the glue soaking in water for twenty four hours so that it can soften and swell. Then heat it in a water bath and apply to the canvas with a brush while still warm (two or three layers) allowing each coat to dry before applying the next.

The priming
Ingredients:
One part of natural plaster or chalk (Spanish white).
One part of zinc white.
Two parts of water.
One part of tepid glue water.
First mix the plaster with the zinc white and the water until you get a creamy but liquid paste. Heat in a water bath and add the glue water. Apply to the canvas while warm and put on three layers, each in a different direction and again letting each coat dry before applying another.

117

Fig. 117.— PRIMING A CANVAS. Put on a layer, going over it three or four times, of rabbit glue, made up of 70 grams of glue per litre of water, while it is warm.

Fig. 118.— Mix one part of plaster (Spar white) with another part of zinc oxide. Add fi 1 to 3 parts of water and one part of sligl warm, liquid glue water.

119

Fig. 119.— Heat the previous mixture in a water bath.

Fig. 120.— Finally apply to the canvas while warm, spreading the paste over the canvas can be done with a brush or a spatula), apply three layers in different directions.

121

Fig. 121.— SUPPORTS FOR OIL PAINTING: 1. Sample of cotton cloth that can be identified by the evenness of the weave. 2. Linen cloth darker than the cotton with a stretch showing some slubbing, is the best surface for oil painting. One of the European manufacturers who gives a guarantee with regard to this is Classens, from Belgium, an old, traditional company of high reputation. 3. Sacking or Hessian. There are a few painters who use it, but they are becoming less, because of the difficulties presented by the coarse texture of the cloth. 4. Cotton cloth of a very simple type, already primed. 5. Standard quality linen cloth, primed. 6. Classens brand linen cloth. Cloth for painting is available in different thicknesses of weave, more or less closely woven, and the best quality is the densest one. 7. Canvas-covered cardboard. 8. Back of a panel of wood of the Tablex type. 9. Plywood. 10. Oak panel (it can be other kinds of wood). 11. Cardboard or wood with white priming. 12. Canvas-covered cardboard with acrylic priming. 13. Thick grey cardboard (it can be prepared with a simple layer of glue, or rubbing with a clove of garlic) and 14. Coloured drawing paper, Canson type.

international stretcher measurements

Stretchers with the canvas already mounted, and cardboard and wooden sheets, are classified according to size by a number which indicates the measurements indicated by the proportions of the picture. Different themes demand the different proportions: *figure, landscape, seascape*. The proportions of the stretchers or pictures corresponding to figure are squarer than those for landscape, and the seascape is the most oblong-shaped (see figures 122, 123 and 124). Note, however, that in practice the artist does not have to stick to this kind of principle. People do paint landscapes on "figure" stretchers and vice versa. Even more: nowadays and always there have been artists who have painted on stretchers of "special sizes".

In any case there is an international table of measurements which is followed by all manufacturers of stretchers with the canvas already mounted, so that the artist can choose one of the sizes from the table, go to the shop and simply ask for: "a figure (or landscape, or seascape) stretcher, number x".

Let it be said that the number of the stretcher generally determines the price of the picture, which means it works in this way: first the number of the stretcher is translated or transformed into points. A number 4 stretcher, equals 4 points, a number 30 stretcher

No.	FIGURE	LANDSCAPE	SEASCAPE
1	22/16	22 × 14	22 × 12
2	22/19	24 × 16	24 × 14
3	27/22	27 × 19	27 × 16
4	33/24	33 × 22	33 × 19
5	35/27	35 × 24	35 × 22
6	41/33	41 × 27	41 × 24
8	46/38	46 × 33	46 × 27
10	55/46	55 × 38	55 × 33
12	61/50	61 × 46	61 × 38
15	65/54	65 × 50	65 × 46
20	73/60	73 × 54	73 × 50
25	81/65	81 × 60	81 × 54
30	92/73	92 × 65	92 × 60
40	100/81	100/81	100 × 65
50	116/89	116 × 81	116 × 73
60	130/97	130 × 89	130 × 81
80	146/114	146 × 97	146 × 90
100	162/130	162 × 114	162 × 97
120	195/130	195 × 114	195 × 97

INTERNATIONAL MEASUREMENTS FOR STRETCHERS

F

P

M

122

123

equals 30 points. Secondly. Each painter, according to his artistic merit, is given a value per point; they say for example that the artist so and so has a value per point of £ 40. The value per point is then multiplied by the number of the picture. For example: the supposed artist whose point is valued at £ 40 will sell a number 40 picture for £ 1,600.

The table of international measurements for stretchers was probably worked out by one of

Fig. 125. — Here is a canvas for painting, mounted on a wooden stretcher. Note that on the stretcher we can see the designation 12F, which means Number 12 canvas, for figures.

125

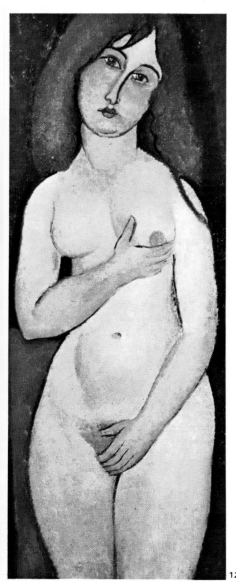

127

126

Fig. 126.— Amadeo Modigliani. "Venus". Private collection. Paris. Modigliani painted this nude on a canvas measuring 160×60 cm., that is special proportions that have nothing to do with the international measurements for stretchers.

Fig. 127.— Pablo Picasso. "In the Lapin Agile (The Harlequin with the glass)". Charles S. Payson collection. Manhasset, New York. The picture measures 99 cm high by 103 cm wide, practically square in shape, which also breaks the rule of the international measurements for stretchers.

128

Fig. 128-— Edgar Degás. "Dance lesson" Louvre Museum, Paris. In principle it seems as though the measurements of the picture correspond to the proportions of a "Figure" canvas, but no; Degás too chose a stretcher with special measurements for this picture: 85×75 cm.

the first canvas manufacturers. This happened approximately 130 years ago. The size of many pictures from the middle of the last century is already in keeping with the measurements of the table shown here. But there were then, and there are now, artists who do without the standard measurements and paint with stretchers that are made to measure, with special dimensions, which correspond, according to them, to a frame specially planned for the main theme of the picture. On this page you can see some examples of unusual sizes in pictures painted by Modigliani, Picasso and Degás. And remember therefore that nothing compels you to paint on prefabricated sizes... although this is usual in 90 per cent of cases.

how to construct a stretcher with canvas

I said, and I repeat, that it is more convenient and safer to buy a ready-made stretcher than to make it yourself, but there are cases where one lives a long way away from where they are sold, or sometimes one throws away a canvas and the stretcher is left empty. In any case it may be useful to know how to make a stretcher and how to mount the canvas.

As you can see in figure 129, as well as the canvas, the four strips of wood to form the frame of the stretcher, the hammer and the saw, you need some small wooden wedges, some special pliers, with wide jaws, to stretch the canvas and a pistol type stapler like decorators use. But we are going to see what you do and how to do it, looking at the series of pictures from figure 130 to 141.

CONSTRUCTION OF THE STRETCHER AND MOUNTING THE CANVAS

Figs. 130, 131 and 132.— The system for assembling a stretcher has two special features. The first is that the strips are thicker at the outer edge than at the inner edge (Fig. 131, A and B). This difference occurs on the upper face of the strips, that is, on the side which will be covered by the canvas, so that the latter will be kept two or three millimetres away from the angle C (Figs. 131, 132) and this angle cannot spoil the picture.

Fig. 133.— The strips are not glued. They are tightly held by the joints, the mounted canvas nailed onto the stretcher and by the wedges which very slightly displace the strips, stretching the canvas and forming a rigid whole.

130

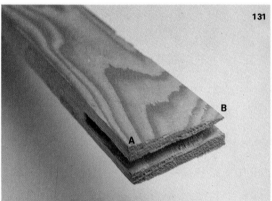

131

132

133

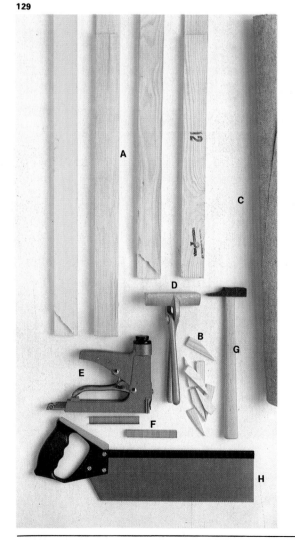

129

Fig. 129.— Materials for constructing a stretcher with canvas. A, strips of wood for the stretcher. B, wooden wedges for stretching the canvas. C, canvas for painting. D, special pliers, with wide jaws, for mounting and stretching the canvas. E, pistol type stapler. F, staples; G, hammer. H, saw.

Fig. 134. With the stretcher already mounted, without the wedges, we cut the canvas, about four centimetres bigger than the stretcher on all four sides.

Fig. 135. With the stretcher and the canvas standing on edge, put the first staple in the centre of one of the longer strips.

Fig. 136.— Turn the stretcher and the canvas over and with the pliers, pull and stretch the canvas and at the same time put the second staple in.

Fig. 137.— Now place the stretcher and the canvas in a vertical position, and put the third staple in the centre of one of the shorter sides Repeat the operation on the opposite side, stretching the canvas with the help of the pliers. At this point the stapling and stretching of the canvas, form a slight wrinkle, which is characteristic of good mounting.

Fig. 138.— Stretching the canvas, still with the help of the pliers, go on putting in staples beside the first, and beside that one, until you reach the stage that can be seen in the following figure.

Fig. 139.— The canvas is now attached to the stretcher and we only have to finish it off at the corners.

Figs. 140 and 141.— The canvas has been folded at the corners and the excess cloth stapled, to finish the mounting. Now it's enough to place and nail the wedges, for the job to be finished.

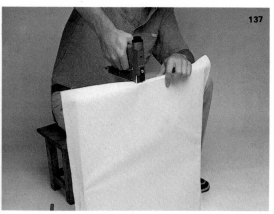

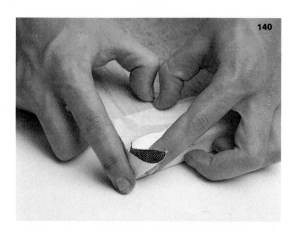

NOTE. Fixing the canvas to the stretcher can also be done with the traditional system of nailing with those small sharp nails with a big head, called tacks.
The system of staples is faster, and it is just as safe when you staple twice, on the edge and on the canvas doubled over the stretcher (Fig. 141); and lastly there is no future problem of rust, something that does happen with the nails.

brushes for oil painting

The brushes normally used for oil painting are made of *hog's hair*. But people also use, for certain areas, brushes made of *sable or squirrel hair*. Not long ago brushes made of *synthetic hair* appeared on the market, but I honestly believe they do not better the hog's hair brush. This is harder and stiffer, it can be scrubbed, rubbed and washed with no danger of the hairs sticking together. The sable or squirrel brush is more suitable for a soft style of painting, with regular layers, without ups and downs but they are also used to deal with the drawing and colouring of small forms or details, fine lines. Brushes for oil painting are made with three forms of point:

1) round pointed brushes
2) brushes with a "cat's tongue" point (filbert)
3) flat pointed brushes (fig. 143)

A brush is made up of handle, metal ferrule and hair. The ferrule is the part which holds the hairs. The handles of brushes for oil painting are long and allow us to hold the brush further up, and paint further away from the picture, with the arms extended, thus extending the angle of vision. The thickness of the hair and, in general, of the whole brush is conditioned by a number printed on the handle which goes from 0 to 24, going up in twos (0, 2, 4, 6, 8, 10, etc.). Below you can see an assortment of brushes which would be considered normal.

142

143

Fig. 142.— Kinds of brushes for oil painting, from left to right, A, squirrel hair brushes. B, synthetic hair brushes. C, sable hair brushes. D, sable hair brush, fan-shaped, especially for blending and very gentle softening of edges.

Fig. 143.— Here are shown three brushes of hog's hair, the kind of hair currently used by the professional painter, in its three characteristic forms: A, with rounded end. B, with "cat's tongue" end, (Filbert) and C, with flat end.

ASSORTMENT OF BRUSHES CURRENTLY USED BY THE PROFESSIONAL

A round brush, sable hair, no. 4.

A flat brush, hog's hair, no. 4.

A round brush, squirrel hair, no. 6.

Two flat brushes, hog's hair, no. 6.

A "cat's tongue" brush, hog's hair, no. 6.

Three flat brushes, hog's hair, no. 8.

One "cat's tongue" brush, hog's hair no. 8.

Two flat brushes, hog's hair, no. 12.

One "cat's tongue" brush, hog's hair, no. 14.

One flat brush, hog's hair, no. 20.

144

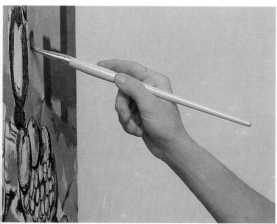

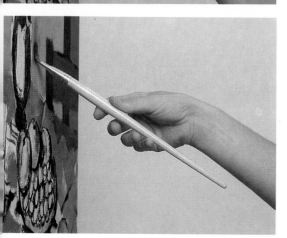

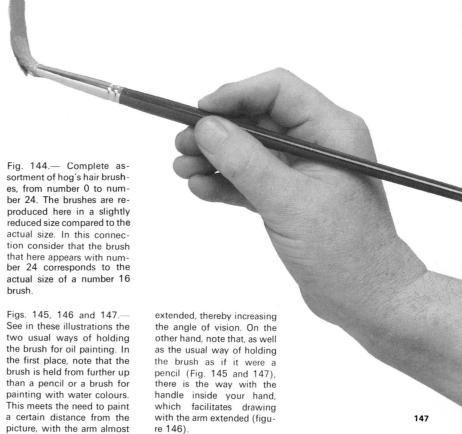

Fig. 144.— Complete assortment of hog's hair brushes, from number 0 to number 24. The brushes are reproduced here in a slightly reduced size compared to the actual size. In this connection consider that the brush that here appears with number 24 corresponds to the actual size of a number 16 brush.

Figs. 145, 146 and 147.— See in these illustrations the two usual ways of holding the brush for oil painting. In the first place, note that the brush is held from further up than a pencil or a brush for painting with water colours. This meets the need to paint a certain distance from the picture, with the arm almost extended, thereby increasing the angle of vision. On the other hand, note that, as well as the usual way of holding the brush as if it were a pencil (Fig. 145 and 147), there is the way with the handle inside your hand, which facilitates drawing with the arm extended (figure 146).

147

preserving brushes

When a brush is old but is in good condition, it paints better than a new one. For this reason and because brushes are expensive, we have to look after them. When one is painting there are no problems. It is even possible to suspend the session for two or three hours without affecting the brushes. But from one day to another, and especially when the picture is finished and you don't intend to go on painting, you have to clean the brushes to leave them as good as new. In this connection, the most practical formula seems to be washing them and rubbing them with turpentine, but it is better to wash them with soap and water. In the picture on this page, figures 148 to 153, you can see clearly the methods for the maintenance and care of brushes.

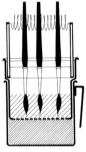

Fig. 148 and 149.— Special container for cleaning brushes. It is a double bottomed pot, and the top layer is full of holes so that when the container is filled with turpentine, the paint that comes off the brushes when they are submerged in it, passes to the real bottom, and the next round of brushes can be washed with relatively clean turpentine. A spring on the upper part of the pot, lets the brushes stay submerged in a vertical position.

149

148

150

152

151

153

Fig. 150, 151, 152 and 153.— One of the most mechanical and tedious jobs a painter has is washing brushes after finishing a session of painting. To put off this job, the professional sometimes resorts to the method of drying the brushes, first with a piece of newspaper and then with a cloth, and leaving them in a pan of water until the next session, the following day, or the day after. But both the previous container and the trick of the water, are only temporary solutions. In the end you have to clean the brushes really well, with the traditional means with water and common soap, twirling the hairs in the palm of your hand, pressing and squeezing them with your fingers running them under water. Then scrub them again on the cake of soap, until the foam is white and the brush is really clean. Smooth out the hairs once they is clean and put the brushes to dry in a pot or jar, with the bristles upwards.

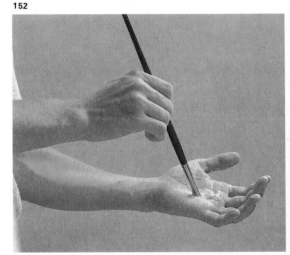

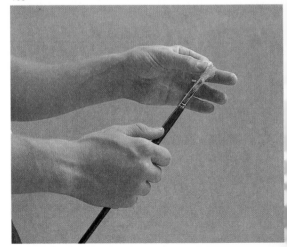

palette knife and painting knives, mahl stick various

As you know a palette and painting knife, has a wooden handle and a metal blade, it is flexible, and ends in a rounded point without an edge. The most characteristic painting knife has the shape of a trowel. They are used to erase, scraping the picture and taking the paint off, and to paint —knife painting— using the knife instead of the brush. Only the stiffer palette knife should be used for removing hardening point from the palette. The mahl stick is a long thin stick topped by a small ball, which is used to rest your hand on when painting small areas, so as not to mark the rest.

In the section on sundries, we list: charcoal for the initial drawing of the picture, spray fixer for fixing the above drawing, pieces of newspaper, rags for wiping and cleaning brushes and a stretcher-carrier, for when you go to paint outside the studio.

154

155

Fig. 154.— Here we have from left to right the range of a mahl stick and six knives, the last of which is made of plastic and can only be recommended for cleaning the palette. Of the five metal knives the one in the middle has the form of a knife and those on either side have the shape of a brick-layer's trowel.

Fig. 155.— Here we have a painter using the mahl stick to outline the shadow of a thin tree trunk, leaning his right hand, which holds the brush, on the handle of the mahl stick.

Fig. 156.—Amongst the different materials needed for painting, it is worth mentioning pieces of newspaper and rags for cleaning the brushes and palette, charcoal, a fixing spray for fixing the drawing initially done with charcoal and a stretcher-carrier which allows you to carry two canvases, so that the freshly painted one does not get spoiled.

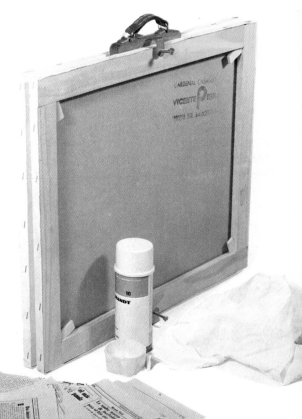

156

solvents and varnishes

Oil colours, just as they come out of the tube, are sometimes too thick. To dilute the colour, make it more fluid, to paint backgrounds, touch up, repair glazes and the like, the artist uses oils, solvents, mediums and varnishes. Here are the most important ones.

Oils

Amongst others we can list linseed oil, poppy oil and walnut oil.

LINSEED OIL: is the best known and widely used of the drying oils for oil painting. It is extracted from the seeds of flax, a plant which also gives us the fibres to manufacture linen canvas for painting. It is light yellow, dries in three or four days, livens up the colours and dilutes the paint well. It is not usually used by itself, but rather mixed with turpentine as we shall see below.

POPPY OIL: is extracted from a variety of the poppy plant. It is a refined oil, practically colourless, used in the manufacture of oil colours. It is very stable, with less tendency to wrinkle than linseed oil, but it dries more slowly. It is the perfect oil for painting glazes.

WALNUT OIL: is obtained by pressing ripe walnuts. It is very fluid, especially for completing painting that requires fine lines, and detailed outlines and finishes. It is similar to poppy oil and like it, is slow to dry.

RECTIFIED TURPENTINE: non fatty, ethereal, volatile liquid, commonly known as turpentine, obtained from distilling resinous balsams that come from a certain variety of pine (coniferous). It is used especially when beginning to paint a picture, when one draws and colours the canvas, with very thin paint. Using rectified turpentine as the only solvent, the paint appears matt, with no gloss. In any case rectified turpentine has to be used in minimum amounts to avoid the paint losing the body needed to adhere to and fix onto the canvas or support. Turpentine is also used to erase painted areas and to clean paint stains on clothes —which should be done before they dry—; it is likewise used to clean brushes, knives and palette, for cleaning your hands, although turps substitute or white spirit can be used for these jobs. It is advisable not to expose turpentine to the sun or it will thicken or become resinous. It is inflammable.

Mediums and Thinners

The medium is an oil paint solvent made up of a mixture of synthetic or natural resins, drying oils and solvents that evaporate slowly or fast. Mediums can be acquired already prepared, in bottles supplied as guaranteed brands such as Talens. But the classic formula prepared by the artist is based on linseed oil and rectified turpentine mixed in equal parts. Apart from this medium which can always be recommended, here we list some of the above mentioned brands:

Fig. 157.— On the market there are more than twenty solvents, oils, essences and varnishes for oil painting. Apart from the fact that you will want to experiment with some of them, I think that in fact the only essential products, are linseed oil, rectified turpentine, a touching up varnish and the final protective varnish. It is also worth getting used to utilising a normal, ready prepared medium, instead of the medium prepared by the artist himself of linseed oil and turpentine in equal parts.

157

NORMAL REMBRANDT MEDIUM made up of resins, drying vegetable oils and slowly evaporating solvent. It can be used at all stages of the work, from beginning to end. It does not present any difficulties or future problems because of an excess or lack of fat or lean.

FAST DRYING REMBRANDT MEDIUM similar to the previous one but faster drying thanks to the incorporation of drying agents and a more volatile solvent. It can also be used at all stages of the picture.

Varnishes

We have to distinguish between retouching varnishes and protective varnishes.

RETOUCHING VARNISH made up of natural or synthetic resin and volatile solvents, it dries fast and keeps the gloss of the picture uniform. For retouching areas that are "soaked in", matt, without gloss, dull in colour, due to absorption of the oil by the lower layers. Repainting these areas with retouching varnish the normal shine returns and the colours revert to their original intensity.

PROTECTIVE VARNISH is the varnish applied to the picture when it is finished and has completely dried. The guarantee of complete and perfect drying presupposes a non-humid period of a year, although this does depend on the atmospheric conditions reigning in the place where the picture is, as well as on the

thickness of the paint. Lastly, it must be said that at present there are glossy and matt varnishes and that they can be found in bottles or in aerosol sprays.

FAT OVER LEAN

So that a painting, with time, does not crack, we have to paint the first layers with more turpentine than linseed oil. Oil paint —and even more so if diluted in linseed oil —is fat. Diluted with turpentine it is lean. A layer of fat paint takes longer to dry than a layer of lean paint. When by mistake lean is painted over fat, the lean layer dries more quickly than the fat layer and when the latter dries, the one on top contracts and cracks, the picture appearing broken up. Paint fat over lean.

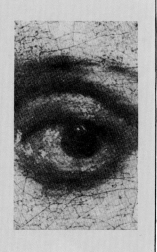

oil colours

There are still people who say that a good painter should make his own oil colours, following the example of the old masters and rejecting the idea of buying them ready made, because the latter do not offer an absolute guarantee of quality and within a few years the colours may turn yellow, the paint may crack and deteriorate. But if you want to verify this in practice, asking experts and famous artists, you will find out that few modern artists make their own oil colours. Almost without exception they buy them ready-made in art shops. This is no obstacle to knowing how and with what one makes oil colours.

Oil colours are made up of two basic ingredients:

A) COLOURS OR PIGMENTS, solid, generally in the form of powder, known as earths, classified as organic when they come from the vegetable or animal kingdom and inorganic, from mineral origins.

These earths are mixed with liquids forming the thick paste characteristic of oil paints. These liquid substances are the

158

B) BINDERS, made up of fatty and drying oils, as well as resins, balsams and waxes.

In the adjoining illustrations you can see the practical aspect of this short explanation. The manufacture at home of oil colours is not advisable nowadays.

We are going to talk of colours (following page) and we are going to study the differences between one white and another white, between colours which dry fast and slowly, with more or less covering power, etc. Something which you need to know to be able to paint with more understanding.

Fig. 158.— According to a picture by Rickaert, drawn by Maurice Bousset, the character who appears in this illustration a 17th century artist, is grinding and making his colours for oil painting, as all artists did in olden times. Rickaert's composition lets us see the small room next to the studio, a kind of kitchen or rudimentary laboratory where the artist of those times carried out all kinds of experiments. This kind of kitchen no longer has any reason for existing, although one still talks of "pictures with a lot of kitchen work", which means a work which, by its texture, subject or treatment, shows up materials, preparation or manipulation out of the ordinary.

159

160

161

162

Fig. 159 to 162.— Home preparation of oil colours. The materials required are: colour, pigment in powder, linseed oil; a slab of glass or marble, a pestle, a palette knife and a container for storing the prepared colour.

Tip the powdered pigment onto the marble slab and pour linseed oil very slowly on top of it while at the same time grinding and mixing the colour with your palette knife until it takes on the consistency and fluidity of oil paint. You have to grind the colour very carefully, eliminating lumps and trying to obtain a homogeneous paste, which may need to be ground for ten minutes or a quarter of an hour and left to be taken up again later, until you have a perfect combination of the colour with the linseed oil.

oil colours

163 **164** **165**

Oil colours are divided into *whites, yellows, reds, greens, blues, browns and blacks*

1. WHITE COLOURS. The most commonly known are lead white (also known as silver white), zinc white and titanium white.
LEAD OR SILVER WHITE. It has extraordinary opacity and covering power, and its speed of drying is also notable. These qualities can be useful for a form of painting based on thick pastes, being equally suitable for backgrounds or first states. It is very poisonous, something which you must constantly remember, especially the artist who wants to make his own colours. Simply inhaling the powder may have serious consequences.

ZINC WHITE. Has a colder tone than lead white, is less compact, covers less and dries more slowly. This last circumstance becomes an advantage when the artist prefers to work on a background which has not dried completely. It is not poisonous.
TITANIUM WHITE. This is a modern pigment in comparison to the two mentioned, it has great covering power, normal opacity and speedy drying and has no serious limitation, which means it is highly considered by most artists.
In oil painting, white is one of the most-used colours, which is the reason why tubes of white oil paint are usually large in size.

Figs. 163, 164, 165.— From left to right. Lead or silver white, zinc white and titanium white. The latter is the most commonly-used by most artists.

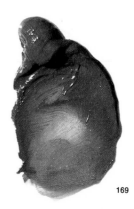

166 **167** **168** **169**

2. YELLOW COLOURS. The most common are: Naples yellow, chrome yellow, cadmium yellow, yellow ochre and raw Sienna.
NAPLES YELLOW. Coming from lead antimoniate, it is one of the oldest colours. It is opaque and dries well. Poisonous like all lead colours, it can be mixed with any other colour

without undergoing alterations, as long as it is pure and of good quality. Rubens used it with preference, especially for flesh colours.
CHROME YELLOW. Derived from lead and therefore poisonous, it is supplied in various shades, from very light, tending to lemon, to very dark, almost orange. It is opaque and dries well, but offers very little resistence to

Figs. 166 to 169. From left to right: Naples yellow, cadmium yellow medium, yellow ochre and raw Sienna.

oil colours

light, tending to become darker over the years, especially the lighter shades.

CADMIUM YELLOW. A good colour, powerful, bright, rather slow drying, can be mixed with all other colours, except those made of copper.

YELLOW OCHRE. It is an earthy colour, classic and ancient with great colouring and covering power, unalterable and can be mixed with any other colour, without presenting any difficulties, as long as it is pure. It is also made artificially without any reduction of the above mentioned qualities.

RAW SIENNA. Just as earthy, with earths coming from Siena (Italy), it is a beautiful, bright colour, but as an oil colour, there is a danger of it turning black because it has to be mixed in a large amount of oil. When painting in oils, therefore, it is better not to use raw Sienna on large backgrounds or large areas where the colour plays an important part.

170 171 172 173

3. RED COLOURS. We can list the most used; burnt sienna, cinnabar vermilion, cadmium red, and crimson madder.

BURNT SIENNA. Similar characteristics to the above-mentioned raw sienna, darker with a reddish tendency, it can be used in all techniques without limitations, that is to say, with less risk of later turning black. It was very much used by the old masters, mainly the Venetians. Some authors maintain that it was the colour used by Rubens to paint the bright reds of flesh.

CADMIUM RED. Substitutes with advantage for vermilion, as it does not blacken when exposed to sunlight. It is a bright, powerful colour, which can be mixed with all colours, except copper colours, such as opaque green. It covers well but dries with some difficulty. It tends to blacken when exposed to the sun. It is not advisable to mix it with copper colours, or with lead white.

CRIMSON MADDER. Very potent colour, supplying a rich range of pinkish, purple and crimson tones. It is rather fluid and dries slowly.

4. GREENS AND BLUES. The following are currently used; terre verte, permanent green, emerald green, cobalt blue, ultramarine blue and Prussian blue.

PERMANENT GREEN. A pale, liminous green colour, produced by the mixture of chromium oxide (viridian or emerald green) and cadmium lemon yellow. It is a safe colour, without limitations.

TERRE VERTE. A colour derived from ochre, with a brownish, khaki green. A very old colour which can be used in all techniques, dries relatively well and has good covering power.

EMERALD GREEN. Known too as viridian green, it must not be confused with Schweinfurt green or opaque green, which in turn is called on some colour charts "emerald green". The latter offers many inconveniences and limitations. This is not so with the emerald green we are referring to —viridian green— which is considered the best of the greens for its tonal capacity and richness, its stability and safety.

COBALT BLUE. It is a metallic colour, non poisonous, which may be used in all techniques, without limitations. It covers well and dries fast, the latter a quality which may be a disadvantage when it is applied on top of layers of paint that are not quite dry, thereby causing cracking. In oil paint, due to the

Figs. 170 to 173.— From left to right, burnt sienna, cinnabar vermilion, cadmium red and crimson madder.

oil colours

174 **175** **176** **177** **178**

Figs. 174 to 178. From left to right permanent green, emerald green, dark cobalt blue, dark ultramarine blue, and Prussian blue.

amount of oil it needs, it may take on a slight greenish tone with time. It is obtainable in pale and dark shades.

ULTRAMARINE BLUE. Like the previous one, this is a colour used since ancient times, coming from lapis lazuli, a semi precious stone, and the reason why it used to be the most expensive colour. At present it is made artificially, and is stable with normal opacity and drying. It is also available in pale and dark shades and in any case shows a more reddish tendency than cobalt blue.

PRUSSIAN BLUE. Also called Paris blue, it is a colour of great staining power, transparent, which dries well and which has the most important defect that it is affected by light, which may fade it (with the peculiarity that the colour regenerates when it is left again in darkness for some time). It is not advisable to mix it with cinnabar vermilion or with zinc white.

5. BROWNS. The most often used are raw and burnt umber, and Cassel earth or Van Dyck brown.

RAW AND BURNT UMBER. Both colours are natural earths, the second being the product of calcination. They are both very dark, and in the raw umber there is a slight greenish tint, while in the burnt umber the tone is slightly more reddish. They can be used in all techniques, but it is inevitable that they blacken with time. They dry very fast, which means it is advisable not to apply these colours in thick layers, to avoid cracks.

CASSEL EARTH OR VAN DYCK BROWN. Of dark tonality, similar to the previous ones, but with a rather greyish tendency, it is not recommended for painting backgrounds in oils, because it cracks easily. It can be used in glazes, retouching and in mixtures for rather limited areas.

6. BLACKS. The most well-known are lamp black and ivory black.

LAMP BLACK. A rather cold shade, it is stable and can be used in all techniques.

IVORY BLACK. A slightly warm shade, it gives perhaps a deeper black than the previous one, and is equally useful for all painting techniques.

Figs. 179 to 182. From left to right: raw umber, burnt umber, Van Dyck brown and ivory black.

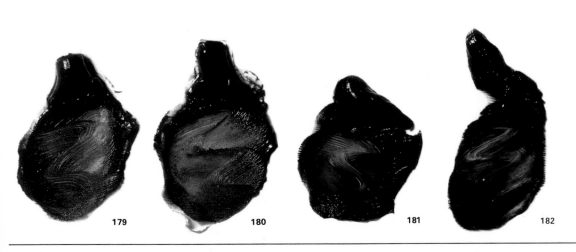

179 **180** **181** **182**

oil colour packings

Oil colours are sold in metal collapsible tubes with a screw cap, in four or five different capacities, and basically in two qualities, the "students" and the "artists" colours.

In the table on this page the sizes and capacities of tubes of oil paints are indicated that are found in art material shops.

Choose an average size and capacity for all the colours, except for white, which we always need to buy in a bigger tube. On this subject, and in accordance with my experience, I recommend:

*tubes of 20 or 30 cc for all the colours,
tubes of 60 cc for white*

The tubes shown on this page, in actual sizes, of bright red (21 cc) Winsor green (30 cc) and titanium white (60 cc), represent this relationship.

Lastly, at the foot of this page are reproductions of six tubes of colours, the three on the left corresponding to students qualities and the three on the right to artists qualities. The latter are undoubtedly better —and more expensive— but the quality of the student-types is perfectly good, especially if you know how to choose the brands.

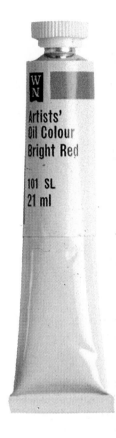

183

Fig. 183.— Three sizes of tubes of oil paint, reproduced in actual size, commonly used by professionals. Note and remember that the tube of white, because it is the one used most, has to be a bigger size.

Fig. 184.— Different brands of tubes of oil paints, within the classes called students (tubes on the left) and for artists (tubes on the right).

	TABLE OF SIZES AND CAPACITY OF TUBES OF OIL PAINT	
tubes	**length**	**capacity**
6	105 mm	20 cm^3
10	150 mm	60 cm^3
13	200 mm	200 cm^3

184

liquid oil colours

185

Not very long, ago, *liquid oil colour* appeared on the market. This is a viscous, semiliquid paint and its characteristics can be summarized as follows:

It is fast to light, dries to touch in a few hours, gives a bright film, can be repainted over after about 6 hours and after a few weeks it can be considered completely dry. With fluid oil colours one can paint on any surface whatsoever, canvas, wood, paper, plastic, glass, and others.

It is recommended to dilute it with white spirit. With this solvent water colour effects can be obtained and it is possible to apply it with an airbrush. Adding a solid agent you obtain a thick colour that can be applied with a knife. Spraying a freshly painted surface with water, you can get special effects.

Fig. 185.— With a collection of 23 colours, in small tins, fluid oil colours, allow us to paint on any surface and are especially indicated for painting large areas of an even colour or tone. Diluted with white spirit (a solvent similar to turpentine), fluid oil colours may be applied with an airbrush, or to create special effects.

Fluid oil paint is appropriate for painting any theme as an opaque point, or, diluted with a solvent, like a water colour. There are, however, some tasks specially indicated for this type or paint. We refer to abstract and mural painting, where there is a need to paint large surfaces with nearly uniform colours.

Fig. 186.— Luis Feitó "Number 935", oils, 1972 (1.60×1.30 m).

Fig. 187.— Joan Ponç "Red

character", oils on canvas. 1967-68 (1.25×1.25 m). The workmanship and theme of both pictures are appropriate for fluid oil colours.

187

186

oil colour chart

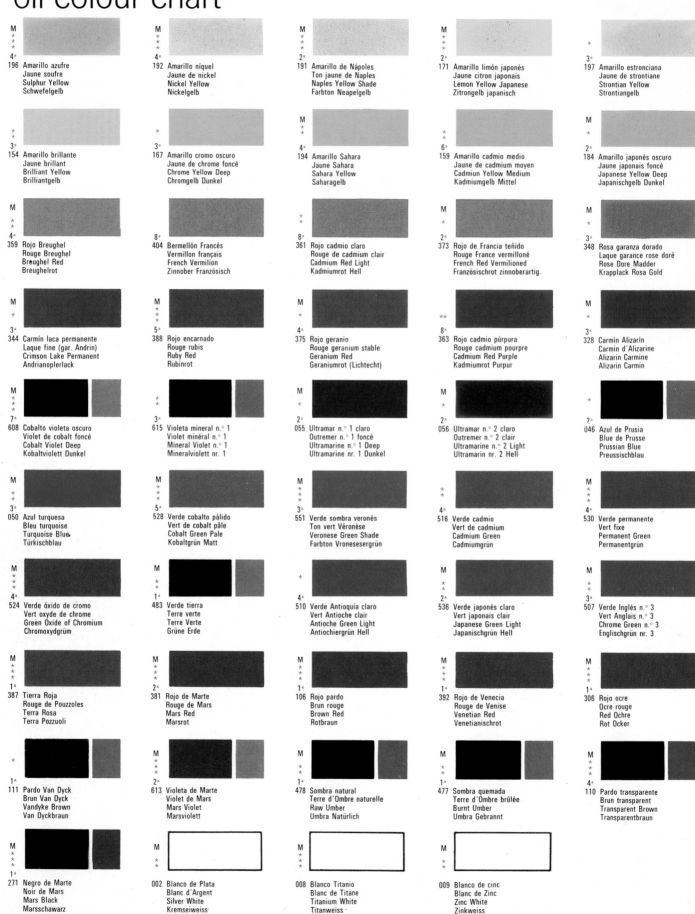

196 Amarillo azufre
Jaune soufre
Sulphur Yellow
Schwefelgelb

192 Amarillo níquel
Jaune de nickel
Nickel Yellow
Nickelgelb

191 Amarillo de Nápoles
Ton jaune de Naples
Naples Yellow Shade
Farbton Neapelgelb

171 Amarillo limón japonés
Jaune citron japonais
Lemon Yellow Japanese
Zitrongelb japanisch

197 Amarillo estronciana
Jaune de strontiane
Strontian Yellow
Strontiangelb

154 Amarillo brillante
Jaune brillant
Brilliant Yellow
Brilliantgelb

167 Amarillo cromo oscuro
Jaune de chrome foncé
Chrome Yellow Deep
Chromgelb Dunkel

194 Amarillo Sahara
Jaune Sahara
Sahara Yellow
Saharagelb

159 Amarillo cadmio medio
Jaune de cadmium moyen
Cadmium Yellow Medium
Kadmiumgelb Mittel

184 Amarillo japonés oscuro
Jaune japonais foncé
Japanese Yellow Deep
Japanischgelb Dunkel

359 Rojo Breughel
Rouge Breughel
Breughel Red
Breughelrot

404 Bermellón Francés
Vermillon français
French Vermilion
Zinnober Französisch

361 Rojo cadmio claro
Rouge de cadmium clair
Cadmium Red Light
Kadmiumrot Hell

373 Rojo de Francia teñido
Rouge France vermilloné
French Red Vermilioned
Französischrot zinnoberartig.

348 Rosa garanza dorado
Laque garance rose doré
Rose Dore Madder
Krapplack Rosa Gold

344 Carmín laca permanente
Laque fine (gar. Andrin)
Crimson Lake Permanent
Andrianoplerlack

388 Rojo encarnado
Rouge rubis
Ruby Red
Rubinrot

375 Rojo geranio
Rouge geranium stable
Geranium Red
Geraniumrot (Lichtecht)

363 Rojo cadmio púrpura
Rouge cadmium pourpre
Cadmium Red Purple
Kadmiumrot Purpur

328 Carmín Alizarin
Carmin d'Alizarine
Alizarin Carmine
Alizarin Carmin

608 Cobalto violeta oscuro
Violet de cobalt foncé
Cobalt Violet Deep
Kobaltviolett Dunkel

615 Violeta mineral n.° 1
Violet minéral n.° 1
Mineral Violet n.° 1
Mineralviolett nr. 1

055 Ultramar n.° 1 claro
Outremer n.° 1 foncé
Ultramarine n.° 1 Deep
Ultramarine nr. 1 Dunkel

056 Ultramar n.° 2 claro
Outremer n.° 2 clair
Ultramarine n.° 2 Light
Ultramarin nr. 2 Hell

046 Azul de Prusia
Blue de Prusse
Prussian Blue
Preussischblau

050 Azul turquesa
Bleu turquoise
Turquoise Blue
Türkischblau

528 Verde cobalto pálido
Vert de cobalt pâle
Cobalt Green Pale
Kobaltgrün Matt

551 Verde sombra veronés
Ton vert Véronèse
Veronese Green Shade
Farbton Vronesesergrün

516 Verde cadmio
Vert de cadmium
Cadmium Green
Cadmiumgrün

530 Verde permanente
Vert fixe
Permanent Green
Permanentgrün

524 Verde óxido de cromo
Vert oxyde de chrome
Green Oxide of Chromium
Chromoxydgrün

483 Verde tierra
Terre verte
Terre Verte
Grüne Erde

510 Verde Antioquía claro
Vert Antioche clair
Antioche Green Light
Antiochiergrün Hell

536 Verde japonés claro
Vert japonais clair
Japanese Green Light
Japanischgrün Hell

507 Verde Inglés n.° 3
Vert Anglais n.° 3
Chrome Green n.° 3
Englischgrün nr. 3

387 Tierra Roja
Rouge de Pouzzoles
Terra Rosa
Terra Pozzuoli

381 Rojo de Marte
Rouge de Mars
Mars Red
Marsrot

106 Rojo pardo
Brun rouge
Brown Red
Rotbraun

392 Rojo de Venecia
Rouge de Venise
Venetian Red
Venetianischrot

306 Rojo ocre
Ocre rouge
Red Ochre
Rot Ocker

111 Pardo Van Dyck
Brun Van Dyck
Vandyke Brown
Van Dyckbraun

613 Violeta de Marte
Violet de Mars
Mars Violet
Marsviolett

478 Sombra natural
Terre d'Ombre naturelle
Raw Umber
Umbra Natürlich

477 Sombra quemada
Terre d'Ombre brûlée
Burnt Umber
Umbra Gebrannt

110 Pardo transparente
Brun transparent
Transparent Brown
Transparentbraun

271 Negro de Marte
Noir de Mars
Mars Black
Marsschwarz

002 Blanco de Plata
Blanc d'Argent
Silver White
Kremseiweiss

008 Blanco Titanio
Blanc de Titane
Titanium White
Titanweiss

009 Blanco de cinc
Blanc de Zinc
Zinc White
Zinkweiss

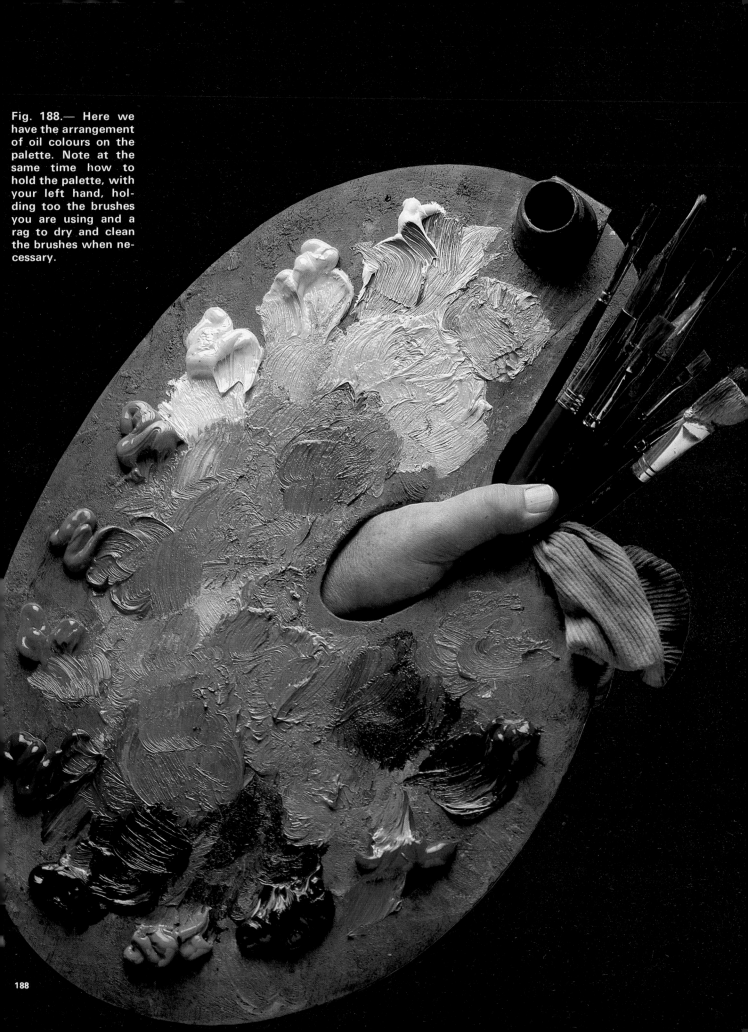

Fig. 188.— Here we have the arrangement of oil colours on the palette. Note at the same time how to hold the palette, with your left hand, holding too the brushes you are using and a rag to dry and clean the brushes when necessary.

* 3ᵃ 165 Amarillo de cromo claro / Jaune de Chrome clair / Chrome Yellow Light / Chromegelb Hell

M ** 2ᵃ 183 Amarillo japonés claro / Jaune japonais clair / Japanese Yellow Light / Japanischgelb Hell

M ** 4ᵃ 195 Amarillo Senegal / Jaune Sénégal / Senegal Yellow / Senegalgelb

** 6ᵃ 158 Amarillo cadmio claro / Jaune de cadmium clair / Cadmium Yellow Light / Kadmiumgelb Hell

* 3ᵃ 166 Amarillo cromo medio / Jaune de chrome moyen / Chrome Yellow Medium / Chromgelb Mittel

** 6ᵃ 161 Amarillo cadmio naranja / Jaune de cadmium orange / Cadmium Yellow Orange / Kadmiumgelb Orange

* 3ᵃ 168 Amarillo cromo naranja / Jaune de chrome orangé / Chrome Yellow Orange / Chromgelb Orange

M **** 4ᵃ 332 Coral / Corail / Coral / Koralle

8ᵃ 402 Bermellón escarlata / Vermillon écarlate / Scarlet Vermilion / Zinnober Scharlach

** 8ᵃ 360 Rojo cadmio naranja / Rouge de cadmium orangé / Cadmium Red Orange / Cadmiumrot Orange

M * 2ᵃ 369 Rojo chino bermellón / Rouge Chine vermillonné / Chinese Red Vermilioned / Chinesischrot, zinnoberartig

M ** 3ᵃ 347 Rosa de garanza / Laque de garance rose / Rose Madder / Krapplack Rosa

M **** 5ᵃ 396 Rojo brillante / Rouge vif / Bright Red / Feurigrot

M ** 4ᵃ 391 Rojo Ucello / Rouge Ucello / Uccello Red / Uccellorot

** 8ᵃ 362 Rojo cadmio oscuro / Rouge cadmium foncé / Cadmium Red Deep / Kadmiumgelb Dunkel

M **** 7ᵃ 627 Violeta cobalto rojo / Violet cobalt rouge / Cobalt Red Violet / Koblatviolett Rötlich

M ** 5ᵃ 603 Violeta de Bayeux / Violet de Bayeux / Bayeux Violet / Bayeuxviolett

M **** 7ᵃ 609 Violeta cobalto sombra claro / Ton violet cobalt clair / Cobalt Violet Light Shade / Farbton Kobaltviolett Hell

** 3ᵃ 616 Violeta mineral n.° 2 / Violet minéral n.° 2 / Mineral Violet n.° 2 / Mineralviolett nr. 2

M **** 4ᵃ 610 Violeta egipcio / Violet d'Egypte / Egypt Violet / Aegyptischviolett

M ***** 3ᵃ 030 Azul cobalto / Bleu de cobalt / Cobalt Blue / Kobaltblau

M *** 3ᵃ 067 Azul real / Bleu rex / Royal Blue / Königsblau

M **** 7ᵃ 027 Azul cerúleo / Bleu céruléum / Cerulean Blue / Cölinblau

M ***** 3ᵃ 062 Azul celeste manganeso / Bleu azural manganèse / Manganese Azure Blue / Mangan-Azurblau

M *** 3ᵃ 033 Azul espacio / Blue espace / Space Blue / Raumblau

M **** 3ᵃ 513 Verde Aubusson / Vert Aubusson / Aubusson Green / Aubusson Grün

M **** 4ᵃ 529 Verde esmeralda / Vert émeraude / Emerald Oxide of Chromium / Chromoxydgrün

M **** 4ᵃ 512 Verde Armor / Vert Armor / Armor Green / Armorgrün

M **** 4ᵃ 518 Verde de China / Vert de Chine / Chinese Green / Chinesischgrün

M * 3ᵃ 553 Verde-vejiga / Vert de vessie stable / Sap Green / Saftgrün (Lichtecht)

M ** 1ᵃ 305 Ocre dorado / Ocre d'or / Gold Ochre / Gold Ocker

M **** 2ᵃ 187 Amarillo de Marte / Jaune de Mars / Mars Yellow / Marsgelb

M ** 1ᵃ 300 Ocre marrón / Ocre brune / Brown Ochre / Dunkel Ocker

M **** 2ᵃ 301 Ocre carne / Ocre de chair / Flesh Ochre / Fleischocker

M **** 3ᵃ 307 Naranja de Marte / Orangé de Mars / Mars Orange / Marsorange

★

** 3ᵃ 775 Amarillo transparente / Jaune transparent / Transparent Yellow / Transparentgelb

** 3ᵃ 777 Rojo transparente / Rouge transparent / Transparent Red / Transparentrot

** 3ᵃ 779 Violeta transparente / Violet transparent / Transparent Violet / Transparent Violett

** 3ᵃ 776 Negro transparente / Noir transparent / Transparent Black / Transparentschwarz

** 3ᵃ 772 Marrón transparente / Ocre brune transpar. / (Brun transparent) / Transparent Brown / Transparentbraun

** 3ᵃ 774 Amarillo dorado transparente / Jaune d'or transparent / Transp. Gold Yellow / Transparentgoldgelb

** 3ᵃ 773 Granate transparente / Grenat transparent / Transparent Garnet / Transparentgranatrot

** 3ᵃ 771 Azul transparente / Bleu transparent / Transparent Blue / Transparentblau

** 3ᵃ 778 Verde transparente / Vert transparent / Transparent Green / Transparentgrün

★ Special colours; but they can be mixed with each other and with all the colours on this chart.

The colours on this chart are printed. There may be small differences from the real colours.

This colour chart has been reproduced and published by special permission from the firm of **Lefranc and Bourgeois.**

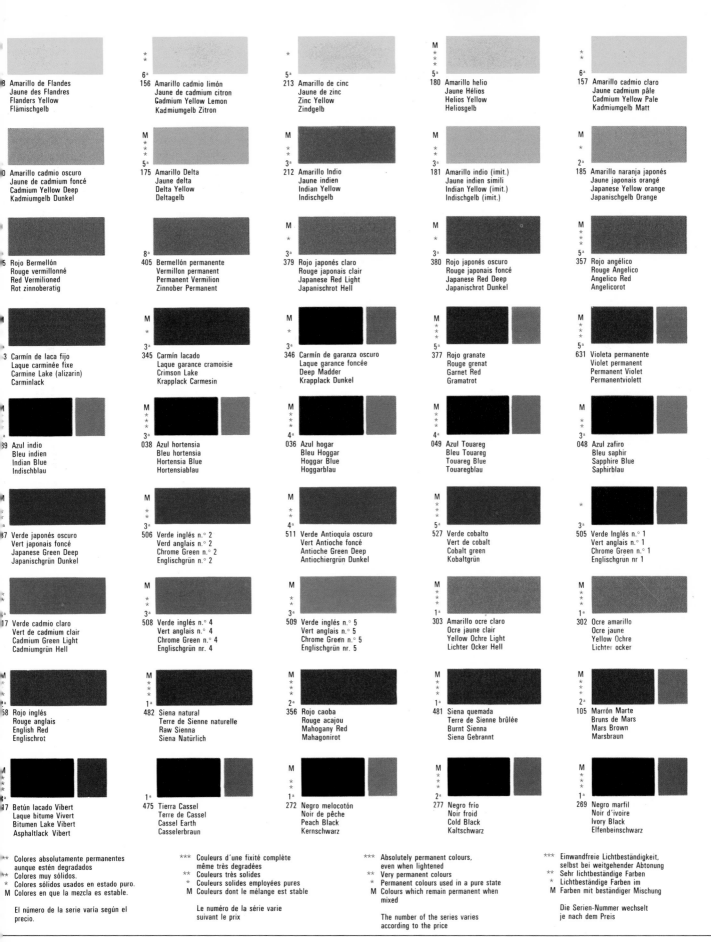

8 Amarillo de Flandes
Jaune des Flandres
Flanders Yellow
Flämischgelb

6ᵃ 156 Amarillo cadmio limón
Jaune de cadmium citron
Cadmium Yellow Lemon
Kadmiumgelb Zitron

5ᵃ 213 Amarillo de cinc
Jaune de zinc
Zinc Yellow
Zindgelb

5ᵃ 180 Amarillo helio
Jaune Hélios
Helios Yellow
Heliosgelb

6ᵃ 157 Amarillo cadmio claro
Jaune cadmium pâle
Cadmium Yellow Pale
Kadmiumgelb Matt

0 Amarillo cadmio oscuro
Jaune de cadmium foncé
Cadmium Yellow Deep
Kadmiumgelb Dunkel

5ᵃ 175 Amarillo Delta
Jaune delta
Delta Yellow
Deltagelb

3ᵃ 212 Amarillo Indio
Jaune indien
Indian Yellow
Indischgelb

3ᵃ 181 Amarillo indio (imit.)
Jaune indien simili
Indian Yellow (imit.)
Indischgelb (imit.)

2ᵃ 185 Amarillo naranja japonés
Jaune japonais orangé
Japanese Yellow orange
Japanischgelb Orange

5 Rojo Bermellón
Rouge vermillonné
Red Vermilioned
Rot zinnoberatig

8ᵃ 405 Bermellón permanente
Vermillon permanent
Permanent Vermilion
Zinnober Permanent

3ᵃ 379 Rojo japonés claro
Rouge japonais clair
Japanese Red Light
Japanischrot Hell

3ᵃ 380 Rojo japonés oscuro
Rouge japonais foncé
Japanese Red Deep
Japanischrot Dunkel

5ᵃ 357 Rojo angélico
Rouge Angelico
Angelico Red
Angelicorot

3 Carmín de laca fijo
Laque carminée fixe
Carmine Lake (alizarin)
Carminlack

3ᵃ 345 Carmín lacado
Laque garance cramoisie
Crimson Lake
Krapplack Carmesin

3ᵃ 346 Carmín de garanza oscuro
Laque garance foncée
Deep Madder
Krapplack Dunkel

5ᵃ 377 Rojo granate
Rouge grenat
Garnet Red
Gramatrot

5ᵃ 631 Violeta permanente
Violet permanent
Permanent Violet
Permanentviolett

39 Azul indio
Bleu indien
Indian Blue
Indischblau

3ᵃ 038 Azul hortensia
Bleu hortensia
Hortensia Blue
Hortensiablau

4ᵃ 036 Azul hogar
Bleu Hoggar
Hoggar Blue
Hoggarblau

4ᵃ 049 Azul Touareg
Bleu Touareg
Touareg Blue
Touaregblau

3ᵃ 048 Azul zafiro
Bleu saphir
Sapphire Blue
Saphirblau

87 Verde japonés oscuro
Vert japonais foncé
Japanese Green Deep
Japanischgrün Dunkel

3ᵃ 506 Verde inglés n.° 2
Verd anglais n.° 2
Chrome Green n.° 2
Englischgrün n.° 2

4ᵃ 511 Verde Antioquía oscuro
Vert Antioche foncé
Antioche Green Deep
Antiochiergrün Dunkel

5ᵃ 527 Verde cobalto
Vert de cobalt
Cobalt green
Kobaltgrün

3ᵃ 505 Verde Inglés n.° 1
Vert anglais n.° 1
Chrome Green n.° 1
Englischgrün nr 1

17 Verde cadmio claro
Vert de cadmium clair
Cadmium Green Light
Cadmiumgrün Hell

3ᵃ 508 Verde inglés n.° 4
Vert anglais n.° 4
Chrome Green n.° 4
Englischgrün nr. 4

3ᵃ 509 Verde inglés n.° 5
Vert anglais n.° 5
Chrome Green n.° 5
Englischgrün nr. 5

1ᵃ 303 Amarillo ocre claro
Ocre jaune clair
Yellow Ochre Light
Lichter Ocker Hell

1ᵃ 302 Ocre amarillo
Ocre jaune
Yellow Ochre
Lichter ocker

58 Rojo inglés
Rouge anglais
English Red
Englischrot

1ᵃ 482 Siena natural
Terre de Sienne naturelle
Raw Sienna
Siena Natürlich

2ᵃ 356 Rojo caoba
Rouge acajou
Mahogany Red
Mahagonirot

1ᵃ 481 Siena quemada
Terre de Sienne brûlée
Burnt Sienna
Siena Gebrannt

2ᵃ 105 Marrón Marte
Bruns de Mars
Mars Brown
Marsbraun

47 Betún lacado Vibert
Laque bitume Vivert
Bitumen Lake Vibert
Asphaltlack Vibert

1ᵃ 475 Tierra Cassel
Terre de Cassel
Cassel Earth
Casselerbraun

1ᵃ 272 Negro melocotón
Noir de pêche
Peach Black
Kernschwarz

2ᵃ 277 Negro frío
Noir froid
Cold Black
Kaltschwarz

2ᵃ 269 Negro marfil
Noir d'ivoire
Ivory Black
Elfenbeinschwarz

currently used oil colours

(Samples supplied by Pelikan brand)

Lemon yellow	Burnt umber	Emerald green
Cadmium yellow medium	Light vermilion	Ultramarine blue deep
Yellow ochre	Deep madder	Cobalt blue light
Burnt sienna	Permanent green	Prussian blue

189

OIL COLOURS COMMONLY USED
BY THE PROFESSIONAL:

*Cadmium yellow lemon
Cadmium yellow medium
Yellow ochre
*Burnt sienna
Burnt umber
Light vermilion

Ultramarine blue deep
Prussian blue
Titanium white
*Ivory black
Deep madder
*Permanent green

Emerald green
Cobalt blue deep

The colour chart reproduced on the previous pages 80, 81 and 82, shows a total of 139 different colours. A lot of colours, aren't there? I suppose no artist paints with so many. Fifteen yellows, seven oranges, twenty reds and crimsons...! Why are there so many yellows, so many reds...? Well, there are artists who prefer Naples yellow, to lemon yellow and there are those who always use chrome yellow —a dark yellow like Kodak yellow—, and never cadmium yellow —a neutral yellow like that of a ripe banana—.

We have to admit that concerning colours there is a diversity of criteria and hence there are these enormous charts, "extensive and confusing", as professor Max Doerner describes them. It is a question of tastes. But there is unanimity at the moment of deciding *how many colours* are necessary. All contemporary and ancient artists work with no more than ten, at the most twelve, different colours apart from black and white. Let us now determine which these ten or twelve colours could be, establishing an assortment for common use. First you must have the three primary colours, yellow, magenta and cyan, corresponding to *a cadmium yellow medium, deep madder and Prussian blue*. Then we need an ochre, a sienna, a red, a green, some other blue... The definitive list could be completed with the colours mentioned in the adjoining chart.

Twelve colours in all without counting black and white. Notice that three of these colours have an asterisk beside them, which indicates the three that could be excluded if you want to reduce the list still more. Lastly note, that white forms part of the essential colours, while black can be excluded, bearing in mind that it can be made up by a mixture of Prussian blue, deep madder and emerald green, or of Prussian blue, deep madder and burnt umber, and all other mixtures.

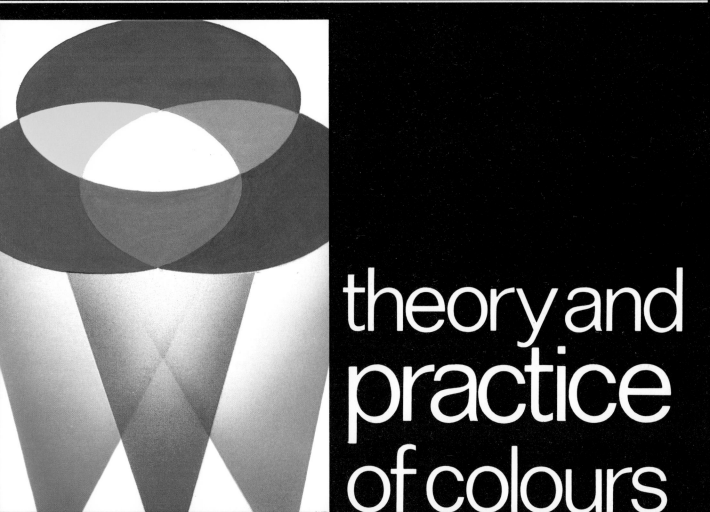

theory and
practice
of colours

light colours

Light is colour.

Any textbook on elementary physics says that light is colour, and proves it by explaining the phenomenon of the rainbow. "The rainbow is the product of millions of drops of rain which, when they receive the rays of the sun, act like millions of small prisms and break the light down into six colours". This textbook on elementary physics also explains that, two hundred years ago, Newton, the physicist, reproduced the same phenomenon of the rainbow in his home: "...he shut himself in a dark room, allowing a pencil of light to come in, similar to a ray of sunlight, and he intercepted this ray with a triangular prism, managing to *disperse* the white light into the colours of the spectrum". The textbook goes on saying that, years later, another famous physicist, Young, did the opposite of Newton: "...Researching with coloured lamps, he determined, by elimination, that the six colours of the spectrum could be reduced to three basic colours: green, red and blue. Then he took three lamps, and projecting three beams of light through three filters with the said colours, he managed to *reconstruct* light, obtaining white light". But for most people, all this, which has been said and repeated, belongs to the world of theory. You and I, are we really conscious of the fact that the light that surrounds us is made up of colours, "travels in a straight line", at a speed of 300,000 kilometres per second and when it arrives at a body, the latter absorbs some colours, and reflects others?

Not me. I have to make an effort to understand it. While considering and analyzing these ideas, one day I decided to put the theory into practice.

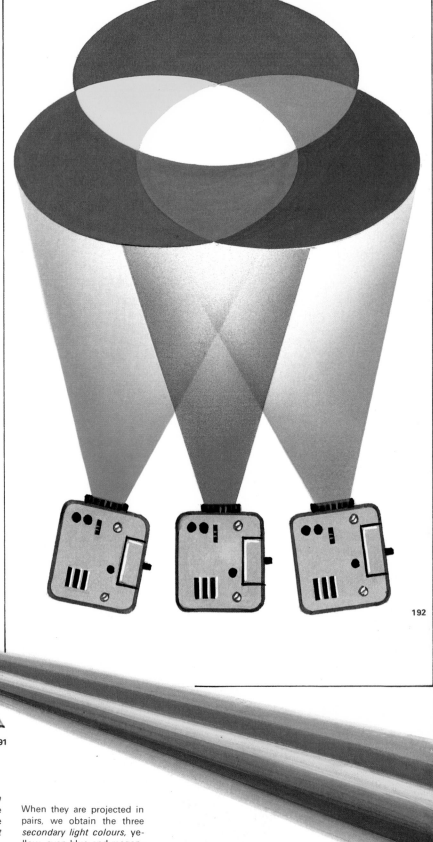

192

191

Fig. 191.— *Breakdown* of light. When a ray of sunlight is intercepted by a triangular prism, the light *breaks down* into the six colours of the spectrum. We have the same effect as with a rainbow.

Fig. 192.— *Reconstruction* of light, projecting three beams of light through three filters, with the *primary light colours*, green, red and blue, white light is reconstructed.

When they are projected in pairs, we obtain the three *secondary light colours*, yellow, cyan blue and magenta.

First, as Newton did, *I broke down* light. I bought a prism, I went home, I shut myself up in the dark, and I projected the little pencil of light and... marvellous —do the same and you'll see it—, the colours of the rainbow were projected onto the wall with a luminosity and clarity that I had never seen! I carried on with my practical experiments and I got .together three slide projectors, to project three beams of light: one green, one red, the other blue.

And then I did what Young did. *I reconstructed* light.

I would need several pages of this book to describe the feelings I lived through that day. For example: to see with my own eyes that projecting a beam of *green light* and projecting on top another beam of *red light*, on the screen I saw the colour YELLOW! Imagine! For me, being a painter, who all his life had painted brown by mixing red and green... But since that day I have begun to understand what light is, which colours make up light, why we see a tomato as being red and a plant as green, why red and green, placed side by side, offer such violence that —as Van Gogh said— "human eyes can hardly bear the sight of this contrast". In other words, from then onwards I understood the true extent of this concept: *light is colour.*

And I developed my own textbook.

Lastly, and admitting —and understan-

Fig. 193.— When a body is illuminated it reflects all or part of the light it receives. A white cube, the same as the page of this book, receives, like all bodies, the three light colours: red, green and blue. But just as they arrive, it returns them, reflects them, providing with the sum of the three, the white colour we see on this page. A black body receives the three colours, which are completely absorbed, leaving the body without light, in the dark, which is the reason why we see it as black. A red tomato absorbs the green and the blue and reflects the red. A yellow banana absorbs the colour blue and reflects the red and green which, together, as we have seen, allows us to see yellow.

—Newton broke down the colours of light and determined the six colours of the spectrum. Young reconstructed light and classified the six colours of the spectrum as primary and secondary:
Primary LIGHT colours:
red, green, blue.
Secondary LIGHT colours: (mixture, in pairs, of the previous primary colours):

blue light+green light=cyan
red light+blue light=magenta
green light+red light=yellow

—from the previous classification we can deduce that a complementary colour is a secondary colour which only needs a primary colour in order to complement it and make up white light (or vice versa).
Complementary LIGHT colours:
Blue, complement of yellow
Red, complement of cyan
Green, complement of magenta

ding— that all the things you and I can see at this moment, are at this very moment receiving the three primary light colours, we establish the physical law of absorption and reflection of the LIGHT colours which says:

All opaque bodies, when they are illuminated, have the property of reflecting all or part of the light they receive.

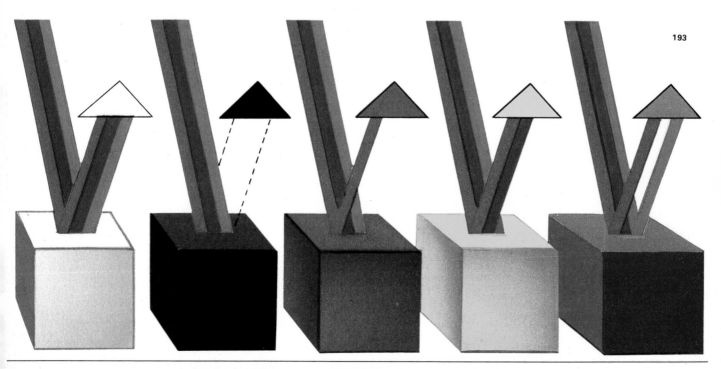

193

pigment colours

PIGMENT colours. Our colours, made with colouring materials and oils and varnishes. With these the artist tries to imitate the phenomena of light and colour we saw on the previous page. In connection with these explanations, remember that light, in order to "colour" bodies, uses *three intense light colours,* which when they are mixed in pairs, provide another *three lighter colours* and which, in the end, make up again the very light, *the colour white,* when they are all mixed together.

But we cannot "colour" with light. Better to say: *we cannot obtain lighter colours with the mixture of dark colours.* Hence, in the same way, taking as a basis the six colours of the spectrum, we change the nature of some colours in respect to others, saying that:

**Our primary colours are the light secondary
colours, and vice versa, our secondary colours
are the light primary ones.**

Complicated? No, let me explain. Our mixtures of colours always suppose *taking away light,* that is, passing from light colours to

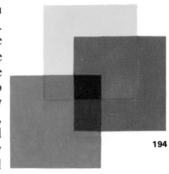

Fig. 194.— The primary *pigment colours,* cyan, magenta and yellow, mixed in pairs supply the secondary ones —green, red and blue. Mixing the three primary colours gives black.

dark colours. If we mix red and green, we get a darker colour, brown; if we mix our pigment primaries together we get black.

Summarizing what I have explained and looking at the pictures at the foot of this page. *The light "colours" by adding colours.* To get the secondary light yellow, light adds red and green, and when their rays are mixed they give a lighter colour. Physicists call this *additive synthesis.*

Pigments colour by taking away colours. To obtain the secondary pigment green, we mix cyan and yellow. In respect to the light colours, cyan absorbs the red, and the yellow absorbs the blue. The only one both reflect is green. This penomenon is called *subtractive synthesis.*

Primary PIGMENT colours

Cyan, Magenta, Yellow

Secondary PIGMENT colours (by mixtures of the previous primary colours in pairs):

**Magenta pigment+yellow pigment=Red
Yellow pigment+cyan pigment=Green
Cyan pigment+magenta
pigment=blue.**

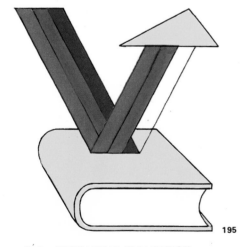

Fig. 195.— *Additive synthesis.* In order to "colour" the secondary light yellow, light adds red and green and takes away (absorbs) the blue.

Fig. 196.— *Subtractive synthesis.* In order to paint the secondary pigment green, we mix yellow and cyan. The yellow absorbs (takes away) the intense blue and the cyan absorbs (takes away) the red. The only colour reflected by both is green.

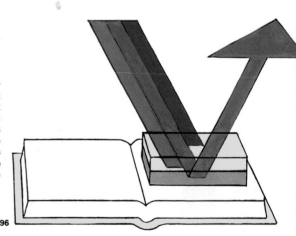

195   HOW LIGHT "COLOURS"

196   HOW PIGMENTS "COLOUR"

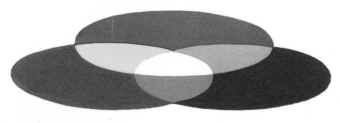

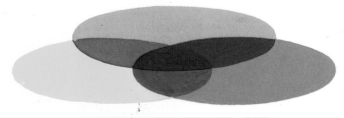

pigment colours

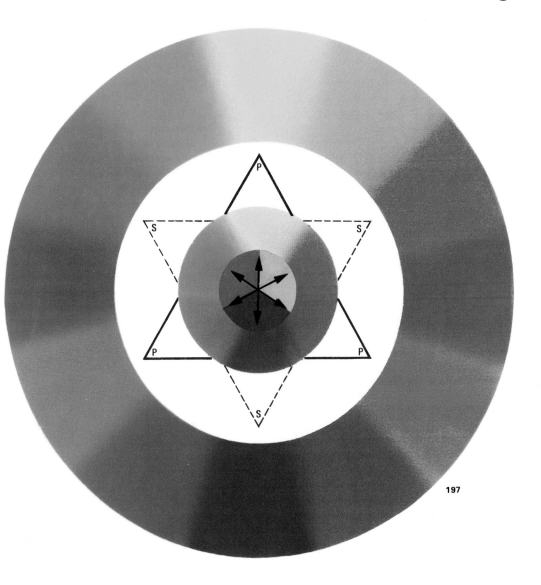

197

Fig. 197.— Chromatic circle or table of pigment colours, where we can see the *primary* colours (indicated with a P in the points of the heavily marked triangle), which mixed with each other in pairs, supply the three *secondary colours* (indicated with an S in the points of the broken line triangle), which in turn mixed in pairs, with the previous primary colours, give six more colours: the *tertiary ones*. Here is the list and classification of these colours.

PIGMENT COLOURS

Primary:

**Yellow
Cyan (1)
Magenta**

Secondary:
**Green
Red
Blue**

Tertiary:

**Orange
Crimson
Violet
Ultramarine blue
Emerald green
Light green**

Now see on this page the chromatic circle or table of pigment colours —our colours—, starting from the three *primary ones,* (shown with a P in the point of the heavily marked triangle) mixing which we obtain the three *secondary ones* (S), which in turn, mixed with the primary ones, provide six more colours calles tertiary.

What has been studied up to here allows us to reach a series of practical conclusions which justify knowing about colour theories:

1. — Light and the artist "colour" with the same colours, the colours of the spectrum.
2. — The perfect coincidence between light colours and pigment colours allows the artist to imitate the effects of the light when it illuminates bodies, and consequently to reproduce

(1) the definition *cyan* does not exist on oil colour charts. It is proper to the graphic arts and colour photography, and has been adopted by the modern treatises of the theory of colour. It corresponds to a blue green or turquoise.

with considerable faithfulness, all the colours of Nature.
3. — In accordance with the theories of light and colour, the artist can paint all the colours of Nature, with only the three primary colours, and
4. — The knowledge and use of the complementary colours allows us to achieve effects of great value for a better resolution of the picture.
We are going to talk about this last conclusion on the following page.

complementary colours

The chromatic circle on the previous page shows us which colours complement each other, placing them in pairs one in front of the other. And so we see that:

Yellow complements **Blue**
Cyan complements **Red**
Magenta complements **Green**
(and vice versa)
Following the same rule of some colours opposing others, we can deduce the complementary colours of the tertiary colours:
Orange complements **Ultramarine Blue**
Light green complements **Violet**
Crimson complements **Emerald green**
(and vice versa)
But what's the real use of the complementary colours at the moment of painting?
In the first place *to create colour contrasts*. If you paint a yellow and right beside it you paint an intense blue you will obtain one of the biggest colour contrasts imaginable in painting. The *postimpressionist* artists like Van Gogh and Gauguin, but especially those who came later —Derain, Matisse, Vlaminck— made of this rule a style of painting, —*fauvism*. Andre Derain's painting "Westminster Bridge", reproduced on the following page, is an excellent example of the possibilities offered by complementary colours when you understand their theory and its practical application.
But, moreover, knowledge of the complementary colours is basic for painting the colour of the shadows, taking into account that, as we will see later, in the proper or projected shadow of any subject the complementary colour of the real colour of the subject in question always plays a part, so that, for example, in the real shadow of a green melon —dark green like the tertiary emerald green—, it is sure that the colour crimson, complementary of this one, plays a part.
The dominion of the complementary colours supposes, in the end, neither more nor less than the possibility of painting with a range of colours of one's own, that is different, based on the **range of broken colours**. A factor that is so important that we will treat it separately, in later pages.

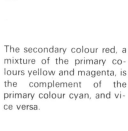

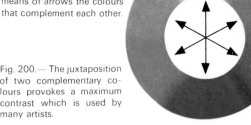

Fig. 198.—Complementary colours.

The secondary colour blue, mixture of the primary colours cyan and magenta is complementary to the primary yellow, and vice versa.

The secondary colour red, a mixture of the primary colours yellow and magenta, is the complement of the primary colour cyan, and vice versa.

The secondary colour green, a mixture of the primary colours cyan and yellow, complements the primary colour magenta and vice versa.

198

Fig. 199.— Here we have the chromatic circle —limited to the primary and secondary colours—, indicating by means of arrows the colours that complement each other.

Fig. 200.— The juxtaposition of two complementary colours provokes a maximum contrast which is used by many artists.

Fig. 201.— As an example of the use of maximum contrasts by the juxtaposition of complementary colours, here we have, on the following page, Andre Derain's picture "Westminster Bridge" (private collection. Paris).

199

200

complementary colours

colour of the subjects

Fig. 202.— See in this apple the factors that determine the colour of bodies, that is the local colour, the tonal colour and the environmental or reflected colour.

202

We say and speak of a blue flower, a red house, a yellow field, and we say it truthfully, but when we are painting not all the flower is blue, nor all the house red, nor all the field yellow. There are shades, penumbras, reflections. There are, in the end, factors which intervene and condition the colour of bodies. They are these:

a) The local colour; its own colour
b) The tonal colour: given by lights and shadows.
c) The colour of the environment: reflection of other bodies.

These three factors are in turn conditioned by:

d) The colour of the light.
e) The intensity of the light.
f) The interposed atmosphere.

The local colour is the real colour of the bodies, in those parts where it is not modified by effects of light and shade or by reflected colours. In the attached figure we see a yellow apple, illuminated by lateral light, located next to a green surface. Well, in this green surface there are no variations. It has no volume, it's flat, its *local colour* is green, there is no other. On the other hand, in the apple, even though it is yellow, and it is lighter on the lighted side, darker on the shadowed side.

In reflects the green of the surface on the side nearest to it. However there is a yellow which is not modified by the lights nor by the shadows, nor the reflections. This is the real yellow of the apple, the local colour.

The tonal colour is a larger or smaller variation of the local colour, generally influenced by the reflection of other colours. Therefore it is a complex colour, with many variations within itself. It is the lightest colour of the illuminated parts, and the darkest colour of the shadowed parts —with an infinity of shades within that— complicated moreover by the colours reflected by other bodies. In the apple in the above mentioned figure we can note the variety of shades of the tonal colour.

The reflected colour is a constant factor, taking into account, on the one hand, the colour of the environment and, on the other, the concrete reflection of one or more certain bodies. In spite of the fact that some artists have made use of this factor as an auxilliary form and sometimes a basic one of illumination, it is not advisable to accentuate the effects of reflected lights and colours, because, in general, they prejudice the volume and the realism of the subject, offering a spurious resolution, that is affected.

203

Fig. 203.— Here we have a graphic example of the *interposed atmosphere* factor, which together with the real colour of the light and the intensity of the light, conditions the colour of the bodies. In this case the apple in the foreground offers greater contrast and greater definition, compared with the more distant apple, which offers less contrast, less definition or clarity and a more bluish, less bright colour.

The proper colour of light influences, naturally, the colours of the model. Early in the morning the countryside is white, grey, blue. In the afternoon towards dusk the same place appears tinted with yellow, ochre, red.

Then it is a question of taking advantage of and interpreting this colour influence to marry and harmonize colours, another aspect which we will talk about in the following pages.

The intensity of the light. Natural light is white. In full daylight bodies appear saturated with colour, they reflect completely their local colour, their own colour. At dusk, logically, the intensity of the colours diminishes. But don't think that this progressive darkness supposes the *blackening* of the colours. Although it is true that the complete absence of light leads to black, it is also true, that *the progressive reduction in daylight leads to a blue light-atmosphere, which tints all the colours with blue.* When the sun goes down and the countryside receives the last light of day, *everything is blue.*

The interposed atmosphere is one of the

Fig. 204.— The intervening atmosphere is clearly visible in the open air, in landscapes which offer distant views, as in this photograph, where the foregrounds stands out as being clearly contrasted and defined, while the mountains in the background lack colour and contrast.

204

factors which offers most possibilities to the artist to represent the third dimension in the picture. The atmosphere exists everywhere. It is air, it's space and its effects may be summarized in the three following factors:

a) *Accentuating the contrast of the foreground compared with the more distant parts;*
b) *Fading and tendency towards grey, as the distance gets further away, and*
c) *Visible clarity in the foreground, in comparison with the more distant parts.*

In the adjoining figure I painted two apples, one in the foreground, the other further away. In the nearer one there is a contrast, a clarity and an intensity of colour which are very well defined. In the one placed further away I have imagined the effects of the interposed atmosphere and I have softened the contrast and clarity factors. As for the colour I have let in blue, eliminated stridency, greying, trying to "paint" space between one apple and another. Effects of interposed atmosphere are perfectly visible in the open air, in the mountain for example, where the foreground offers a marked contrast in tone and colour, while the mountains in the background appear to be grey or light blue.

painting with two colours and white

Theory and practice. We have to alternate learning theoretical factors and rules, with practical exercises in oil painting gradually becoming more complicated, first with two colours, then with the three primary colours—, and finally with all the colours.

For this reason it seems better to me to start from zero, that is, from the supposition that you have not painted often in oils and are practically ignorant of the part of the skill related to fluidity, stickiness, covering quality and how well the colours dry, as well as how these qualities can be used by the artist to cover, cut out and cut out again, draw at the same time as he paints. I think that it is useful to practise this part of the skill without the added problem of knowing how to see and compose colours.

Firstly, then, with two colours and white. These are the colours.

Burnt sienna
Prussian blue
Titanium white

The remaining material and tools consist of:
canvas covered cardboard or simple cardboard
4 no. 10 flat hogs' hair brushes
2 no. 8 flat cat's tongue, hogs' hair brushes
1 flat no. 6 hogs' hair brush
1 round no. 6 sable brush
Medium, painting knife, newspaper pieces, and cloths.

I ask you to begin by painting the samples of colours shown in this figure. In this case it is very important to paint with clean brushes. Here are the mixtures I myself made for this limited range of samples:

Colour no. 1. - White with a little - very little - Prussian blue.

Colour no. 2. - White with a little - very little - burnt Sienna.

Colour no. 3. - Mixture of the two previous colours.

Colour no. 4. - The previous colour with more blue than Sienna.

Colour no. 5. - Colour no. 3 with more Sienna than blue.

Colour no. 6. - The two previous colours mixed in equal parts.

Colour no. 7. - Plain Prussian blue.

Colour no. 8. - Plain burnt Sienna.

Colour no. 9. - A mixture of the two previous colours with somewhat more Sienna, giving an absolute black.

And now let's get on with the cylinder and

Figs. 205, 206 and 207.— Here are the colours for carrying out these first exercises, painting with two colours and white, from left to right, Titanium white, burnt sienna and Prussian blue.

Fig. 208.— It is a good idea for you to make up the colours of these few samples, painting with the three previous colours, in order to capture the chromatic possibilities of burnt sienna, mixed with Prussian blue and both mixed with titanium white.

glass on the following page. Of course, you should paint with real objects. The glass and the saucer are perfectly everyday. For the cylinder you only have to roll up a sheet of white paper to form a cylinder measuring about 6 cm in diameter by 11 high. Place these models on a table, with a sheet of white paper as background.

Both the cylinder and the glass have to be completed at the first try, which means you have to evaluate tones and break down shadows at the first touch of the paint, even using your fingers.

problems of construction; perspective

When I painted the glass half full of water I tried to see tones, different colours within the evenness of the grey. I studied the direction of the brush-stroke —both with the cylinder and with the glass—, trying to cover, and better explain the form. I also considered that it is perfectly valid, when painting glass to accentuate the contrasts in order to highlight the clarity.

209

210

Fig. 209.— I painted these objects from the natural state, with daylight or artificial light, considering that the light had to be lateral and to come from above. I painted on a canvas covered cardboard, but there's nothing to stop you painting on cardboard, or even on well sized thick drawing paper, of the Canson type, for example.

Fig. 210.— Painting a glass object may seem to be a complicated problem, because of the forms, shadows and colours caused by and conditioned by the transparency factor. In reality, and as Michelangelo said, it's a matter of "stupidly copying everything". And be careful with the colour, take into account that these slight, very slight variations between greys with a bluish tendency and greys with a burnt sienna tendency, are those which enrich and give value to these simple models.

construction

211

212

Fig. 212.— Take the pencil within your hand, drawing as a sketch, with a wedge-shaped lead, to achieve wider lines.

Fig. 211.— A cup of coffee, a sherry glass, a tumbler, a mug of beer, a salt shaker... Any one of these subjects is useful as a model to draw and "practice" for studying shadows, transparencies, volumes. Draw with a pencil that has a thick lead, a lead in the form of a fat wedge, which will allow you to draw greynesses and breakdowns like these, wide, full, unworried and spontaneous.

And now we are going to paint a simple still life, still painting with two colours and white. But beforehand, as a previous exercise in drawing and construction, I ask you to draw with lead pencil some odd things like these, which can be found in everyone's house. A cup of coffee, a glass of sherry, a tumbler, a mug of beer, a salt shaker... Choose these or similar objects, draw from the natural state, planning to fill up five or six sheets of drawing paper. Work with a soft pencil such as 3B or 4B and with a medium grain drawing paper. Draw with the pencil inside your hand, draw with the lead in a wedge form so that your lines are thicker (figs. 211 and 212).

problems of construction; perspective

The laws of perspective cannot be forgotten. On these depend whether the picture is constructed well or badly, especially in cases including geometrical forms. Luckily in this case the problem comes down to placing a series of circles in perspective, looking at them from above or below, which is regulated by the so-called parallel or one point perspective, the least complicated form of perspective, as you can see in the short explanation given in the adjoining box. See also, in the illustrations and texts at the foot of the page, the rules to be taken into account when constructing circles and cylinders in correct perspective. Remember that we are dealing with practice, and it would be a good idea to follow these explanations with a pencil in hand, drawing.

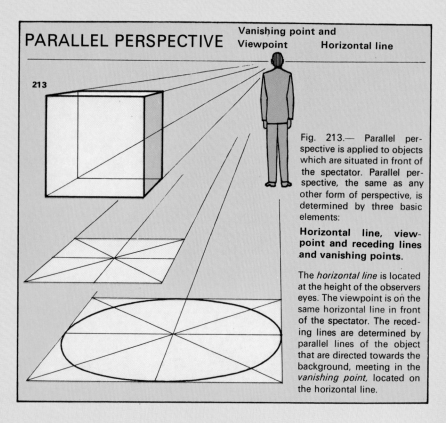

PARALLEL PERSPECTIVE

Vanishing point and Viewpoint — Horizontal line

213

Fig. 213.— Parallel perspective is applied to objects which are situated in front of the spectator. Parallel perspective, the same as any other form of perspective, is determined by three basic elements:

Horizontal line, viewpoint and receding lines and vanishing points.

The *horizontal line* is located at the height of the observers eyes. The viewpoint is on the same horizontal line in front of the spectator. The receding lines are determined by parallel lines of the object that are directed towards the background, meeting in the *vanishing point,* located on the horizontal line.

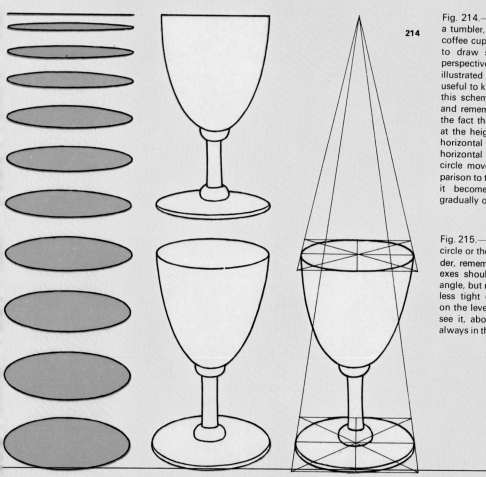

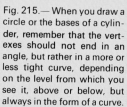

214

Fig. 214.— In order to paint a tumbler, a wine glass or a coffee cup, you do not need to draw such a laborious perspective scheme as is illustrated in this figure. It is useful to know however that this scheme exists, to learn and remember, for example, the fact that a circle located at the height or level of the horizontal line, appears as a horizontal line, while, as the circle moves lower in comparison to the horizontal line, it becomes an oval that gradually opens up.

Fig. 215.— When you draw a circle or the bases of a cylinder, remember that the vertexes should not end in an angle, but rather in a more or less tight curve, depending on the level from which you see it, above or below, but always in the form of a curve.

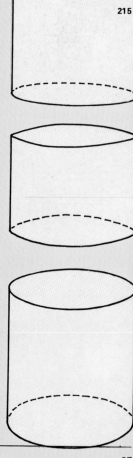

215

previous study in lead pencil

Fih. 216.— Objects that are easy to find and to compose, a bottle of cognac, a cup of coffee with saucer and spoon, and a glass of cognac. All placed on a table against the wall with the background a sheet of white paper curved as shown. (see plan 216A).

It is a good idea to carry out a previous study in lead pencil, to know the subject better. You can study the forms, dimensions and proportions, the colouring, the play of light and shadow.

216

216 A

first stage

Fig. 217.— I did this painting on a number 3, figure, canvas covered cardboard. The drawing turned out slightly bigger than it is reproduced on this page. Of course, we continue with the idea of painting this still life with two colours and white. In this illustration we can see the initial sketch drawn in charcoal, which was fixed with liquid fixer sprayed on when it was finished.

217

second stage

Fig. 218.— As you can see in this picture the painting was done by applying the techniques of direct painting (alla prima) that is to say, completing it in areas and at the first attempt, but still retaining the possibility of rectifying forms and colours as the picture progresses.

218

last stage

Fig. 219.— The result of this simple but educational exercise, painting in oils with burnt sienna, Prussian blue and titanium white. On the basis of this interesting experiment, we can now talk of painting in oils with more colours, so that we can capture all the colours of nature.

use and abuse of white

In some of my books, but mainly in the one called *This is how to paint*, I have discussed pictures that are sadly grey, without contrasts, dull, monotonous colours, with no appeal, and I said —that is in the same book— that one of the main reasons why the amateur falls into what I call "the trap of the greys", is the use and abuse of white and black mixed with other colours. He believes that to lighten a colour you only have to add white, and to darken it to add black... without taking into account that with black and white you are really painting grey.

Note that this does not happen only with the inexperienced amateur. On a lesser scale I have seen the effects of the "grey trap" in more than one exhibition of pictures. Mental laziness on the part of the artist? Maybe, but in any case let me remind you of the following facts.

Painting in water colours, white does not exist. Water colours are transparent, and to paint sky blue you only have to add more water to the blue, so that the white of the paper shows through more and the blue is lighter. Painting in oils, white is a "colour", and oils are opaque. To paint sky blue you have to mix blue paint with white *paint*. White *paint* is a basic component —50% together with black— in getting a grey.

Adding white to a colour involves in theory —and unfortunately in practice— moving this colour in the direction of grey.

Do you know the experiment with white coffee? If you take two identical white cups with the same amount of coffee in both, and add water to one of them and milk to the other, you will be able to see that the water lightens the colour of the coffee turning it towards red, orange, gold..., reacting in a similar way as when you mix a transparent colour like water colours with water. In the other glass, the milk transforms the colour of the coffee into a dirty Sienna, a dirty ochre, a grey cream... behaving in the same way as when you mix the *colour* white, an opaque *colour* with another equally opaque colour. The experiment enables us to understand and remember a highly important rule, that is:

> *White is not the only way*
> *to obtain a lighter colour.*

In this too, we have to imitate nature. In this respect, observe how the colour red behaves in the spectrum (fig. 224C). Note that when it gets dark it turns violet and blue, and when it gets lighter it first turns towards orange and

Fig. 220.— Two glasses with the same amount of coffee, one lightened with water and the other lightened with milk, offer results that can be compared to painting in water colours or in oils. The water colour, on being lightened with water, keeps its original tone. The oil colour, opaque, when lightened with the *colour* white, has its original tone adulterated, and made grey.

then towards yellow, so that in order to lighten a red, first you have to mix it with yellow, and then with yellow and white. Try it Paint something red —a tomato or a pepper— and try to lighten it "whisking the white out of sight" as my old art teacher used to say.

As for black, the problem is the same but

221

more dramatic. The Impressionists reached the point of excluding black from their palettes, because they considered it the enemy of colour.

But let us talk about black on the next page.

Fig. 221.— The illuminated parts of a red pepper or tomato, should not be lightened, just with white, pinkish colours or mixtures of white and red. The light parts of red bodies, have to be obtained, following the scheme of the spectrum, with oranges, and yellows... which in some areas may be mixed with white. But try, as far as possible to ''whisk the white out of sight'' knowing that, in a fatal way, white alters the saturation, makes the colours grey.

use and abuse of black

Yes, Manet excluded black from his palette. And Monet, and Degás, and Sisley, and Cézanne.

Years later, once the fever of Chevreul, the colour theoretician, had passed, Van Gogh and Gauguin and Bonard used it again —black, of course—. But they did it with insight, they used it as *local colour*, as a proper colour, not as a *tonal colour* —are you following me? That is to say, they did not use black as a "colour" to darken shadows, because in this they already has the experience of their prodecessors, Monet, Manet, Degás, and others. Because they all knew perfectly well that.

In Nature black does not exist

In fact, black is the negation of light. A black surface absorbs all the light colours and does not reflect any. The colour black in oils —*ivory black or lamp black or jet black*—, mixed with any other colour, to darken and paint in shadows, becomes a germ of dirtiness which contaminates all colours, taking life away from them, transforming them automatically to a horrible grey range.

Make the test yourself. Take yellow oil paint —cadmium yellow, for example—, and paint a strip, then try to darken the yellow with black, painting a breakdown like the one on the following page (figure 224A). Do you see what happens? The black does not darken the yellow: it dirties it, it turns it green, a strange green which in no way represents the good shadow of the colour yellow. Let's go back to nature and try to imitate once again the behaviour of the spectrum seeing that darkness comes from the side of the reds, that these become oranges, and lighten until they are yellow. So that the perfect range of a broken down yellow should begin with black, followed by purplish red, Sienna, orangish Sienna, chrome yellow, cadmium yellow, lemon yellow (mixture of yellow, green and white) and finally white. (See on the right, above, a scheme of the spectrum and below, in figures 224A BAD and 224B GOOD, two schemes of the colour yellow broken down with just black and with the above mentioned colours of the spectrum).

Confirming this theory see what I have painted so that you will forget black as the colour of shadows. Here on the right 222, and above (fig. 222 BAD) a yellow jar and a yellow banana, painted exclusively with cadmium yellow medium, black and white,

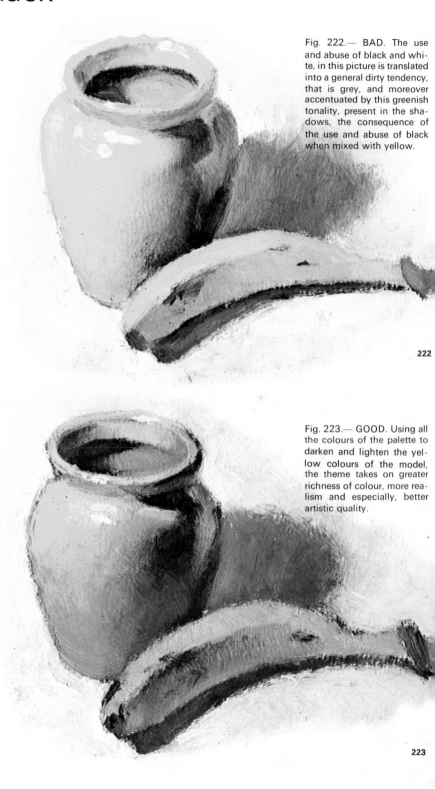

Fig. 222.— BAD. The use and abuse of black and white, in this picture is translated into a general dirty tendency, that is grey, and moreover accentuated by this greenish tonality, present in the shadows, the consequence of the use and abuse of black when mixed with yellow.

222

Fig. 223.— GOOD. Using all the colours of the palette to darken and lighten the yellow colours of the model, the theme takes on greater richness of colour, more realism and especially, better artistic quality.

223

Fig. 225.— Here we have three formulas for making up a neutral black, a warm black and a cold black, with the mixture of the colours burnt umber, emerald green and deep madder and Prussian blue.

with a completely unpleasant result, that is cold, colourless, monotonous and dirty.

Below, the same subject painted with the above mentioned range (fig. 223 GOOD), with a palette of reds, siennas, ochres, crimsons, blues... and white —but very little—.

Lastly, note that in the schemes of the spectrum, as well as the yellow and the red that we have already studied, we offer the one corresponding to the colour blue, and prove that on the side of clarity, blue meets with green, while on the dark side it finishes with this intense, dark blue, of a violet tendency, represented in colour charts by the colour blue, *ultramarina blue*. Let us then see that in a breakdown of the colour blue there should be a bluish-green tendency in the light parts, neutral in the centre and violet in the dark parts.

And in connection with black, see at the foot of this page, the three classical mixture formulas for making up the colour black... without black:

Formula A): neutral black:
  1 part of burnt umber
  1 part of emerald green
  1 part of deep madder

Formula B): warm black:
  1 part of deep madder
  1 part of burnt umber
  1/2 part of emerald green

Formula C): cold black:
  1 part of burnt umber
  1 part of Prussian blue
  1/2 part of emerald green

What does "warm black, cold black" mean? Well... a black with a tendency towards crimson, suitable for painting the black of a doorway or a window of a building in full sunlight —of a reddish tendency—; or to paint the black of an intensely dark area in the middle of a wood —of a bluish tendency—.

224

224A BAD

224B GOOD

224C BAD

224C GOOD

224D BAD

224D GOOD

225A BAD

225B GOOD

225 C

the colours of the shadows

Each artist has his own palette and nobody sees colours in the same way.

What does not admit of variations, where painting has to submit to a perfect *colouring relationship* is in the shadows. With reason Rubens said: "It doesn't matter what colour you give the lights, if you paint the shadows with the colour corresponding to each light." But what is the colour of the shadows?

Some time ago, when I was holding classes of painting and drawing in the Escuela Massana in Barcelona, I found a formula which since then I have recommended to hundreds of pupils. It is based on generalizing the colours which play a part in any shadow colour. These are the three colours.

1. *The colour itself in a darker tone*
2. *The complement of the colour itself*
3. *The colour blue, present in every darkness*

Let's talk with examples. On this page and on the page on the right, there are various schemes painted with the three colours which play a part in the colour of shadows. See the still life in figure 229 —a dish, four apples and two bananas—, reproduced three times on a small scale in figures 229 A, B and C. Now look at what the pictures "say":

Fig. 229 A); The colour itself in a darker tone; is the *tonal* colour, ochre in the shadow of the dish, dark yellow in the shadows of the bananas, dark red for the apples. These colours, mixed with...

Fig. 229 B): ... the complement of the colour itself. In the dish and the bananas, both yellow, the complementary colour is intense blue; in the apples, which are red, the complementary colour is green... These colours mixed with...

Fig. 229 C): ...blue, provide the colour of shadows.

Keep in mind that blue is the basic colour of the shadows. Decide yourself, looking at the subject, whether this blue has to be clean, neutral, like cobalt blue, or has to be greenish, like titian blue, or has to be a purplish blue like ultramarine blue.

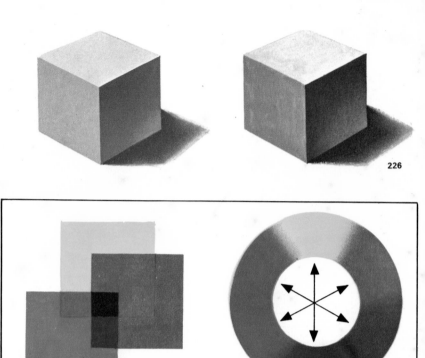

226

227

Fig. 227.— REMEMBER. Yellow, magenta and cyan, are the primary colours which mixed in pairs provide the secondary colours: green, red and blue.

Forming a circle with these colours, we can establish the complementary colour of each in respect of the other. For example, the complement of yellow, is blue.

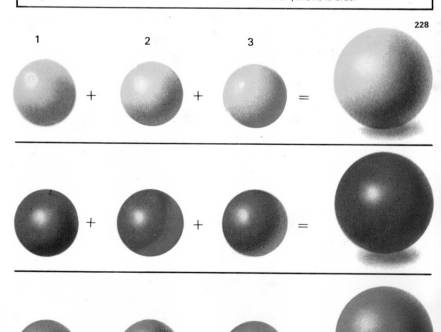

228

1   2   3

Fig. 228.— The colour itself in a darker tone, mixed with the complementary colour, mixed with blue, provides the colour of the shadow. See this formula applied to a yellow object, a red object and a blue object.

229   A   B   C

Fig. 229.— Here we have a still life where the basic colours are the yellow of the bananas and the dish, and the red of the apples. In the pictures at the top of the page (229, A, B and C) see the theoretical-practical separation of the colours that make up the shadow. In figure 229 A, I have painted the shadows the complementary colour of the colour itself, and in figure 229 C, there is the blue which plays a part in the colour of shadows. In connection with this blue it is worth quoting Monet's phrase when he was talking with his friends about the colour of shadows. "When it gets dark the whole country turns blue", or what is the same thing, when the light diminished in the parts in shadow the influence of the colour blue increases.

harmonizing colours

In all the pictures of the great masters there is always a planning of colour which answers, on the one hand, to what the subject itself explains and, on the other, to a harmonization of tones and colours that is calculated and organized by the artist himself. It is not by chance that Rubens painted the flesh, the faces and bodies of his models, always with a range of warm colours, with pinks, yellows, ochres, oranges and reds, while his friend Velázquez painted the flesh, the faces and bodies with greys, bluish pinks, "dirty" yellows, greenish ochres, that is to say, with a range of less warm, almost cold, colours. Harmonizing colours is an art and is an important part in the art of painting. A picture may be pitched with colours of a reddish tendency, answering to a *range of warm or hot colours*. Or it may be painted with bluish colours, answering then to a *range of cold colours*. Likewise it may offer a series of greyish tones and colours, answering to a range of broken colours. It is even possible to paint with a *melodic range of colours,* understanding that such a range is made up of a dominating colour broken down in different tones, just as Picasso did in the pictures of his blue epoch or his pink epoch (fig. 230).

Luckily these ranges of colours are given by the subject itself, thanks to the fact that in nature there is always, whatever the theme, a *luminous tendency* which relates some colours with others and them all to each other. In the adjoining figures, numbers 231, 232 and 233, there are three examples of luminous tendencies offered by Nature itself. In figure 232 you can see a seascape painted on the fishermen's wharf in Barcelona, with a range of cold colours. It was ten in the morning on a winter's day, with the sun half covered by the clouds, lighting against the light, so that the seawater, with hardly any waves, was like an almost white mirror, in which the grey and blue reflections of the ships and boats tied up to the wharf appeared. Everything was grey and blue. There was nothing else to do but take in and see, almost become obsessed with the idea of blue, in order to get this result. At the other extreme (figure 233), we have a street in a village, painted at five o'clock in the afternoon on a warm summer's day, with a range of warm colours. The sun at this time "colours" with warm colours, yellows, ochres, Siennas, reds. See this wide range of yellows and ochres reflected by the walls of

230

Fig. 230.— Pablo Picasso "The meeting". Picasso Museum. Barcelona. The picture belongs to Picasso's famous "blue period", when the artist enjoyed himself painting with a *melodic range of colours,* based on the colour blue.

the houses, where even the blue shadows offer a reddish, purplish tendency.

Lastly, see in figure 231, a still life painted in the studio, with daylight, painted with a range of broken colours, offering a neutral colour tendency, neither warm nor cold, product of mixtures between complementary colours and white. A very interesting formula which we are going to talk about in the following pages.

Artificial light also offers a definite chromatic tendency. The light of a normal electric lamp is yellowish. Fluorescent light is bluish or pink.

Now that we are in the field of practice, the artist should first study, before painting, the luminous tendency presented by the subject. In the second place, once the range of colours he is going to use has been decided on, he has to enjoy this tendency, accentuate it, if suitable, and with this he will be on the way to interpreting the colour, and to painting a good picture.

231

Fig. 231.— J. M. Parramón "Still life with lemonade". Private collection. Here we have an example of harmonizing colour, by means of a range of broken colours, offered by the hues and tones of the model itself.

232

Fig. 232.— J. M. Parramón. "The fishermen's wharf in the port of Barcelona". Private collection. The harmonization of the colour is generally given by nature itself. At the time and the season of the year when I painted this picture, at ten in the morning on a winter's day, with the sun almost hidden by clouds, the scene offered this range of cold colours, perfectly harmonized.

233

Fig. 233.— J. M. Parramón. "La Torra". Private collection. Five o'clock in the afternoon on a summer's day, with sun and a clear sky. At this time of the day and year the light is rather orange, yellow, with a red tendency. Nature herself harmonized the colours, "tints" the forms and the bodies with a golden colour. Harmonizing, in short, is the same as knowing how to see, interpret and highlight these effects of light and colour, even when they are not as obvious as in this case.

range of warm colours

234

Fig. 234.— This palette shows the range of warm colours, reminding and explaining that the dominating colour is red, and the related colours are green-yellow, yellow, ochre, crimson, purple and violet.

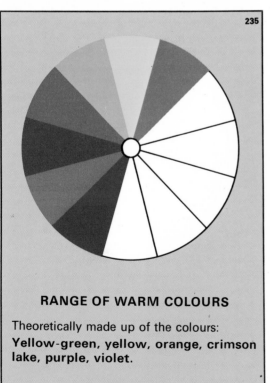

235

RANGE OF WARM COLOURS

Theoretically made up of the colours:
Yellow-green, yellow, orange, crimson lake, purple, violet.

From a theoretical point of view the range of warm colours is made up of the colours shown in the chart (fig. 235). In practice, thinking of the colours that are close to, or related to red, and taking into account the colours currently used by the professional, reproduced on the palette shown here (fig. 234), we have to choose the colours:

yellow, ochre, red, burnt umber, deep madder, permanent green, emerald green and ultramarine blue.

But, be careful! The fact that we have excluded cobalt blue and Prussian blue does not mean that these colours —and all colours— cannot play a part in a range of warm colours. *Range of warm colours* means chromatic tendency towards red, yellow, orange, ochre, sienna... but still being able to mix these and other warm colours with blues, greens, purples, to make them greyer, "to dirty them" —as Titian said— in order to paint shadows and penumbres.

Fig. 236.— Paul Cézanne. "Still life from the curtain" (fragment). Leningrado, Museum of the Hermitage. Here we have a superb example of how Cézanne applied a range of warm colours. Study this colouring to see how by means of yellows, reds and siennas, Cézanne achieves an extraordinary harmonization of colour.

range of cold colours

Fig. 237.— Symbolic palette showing the range of cold colours, which as you can see offer a dominating blue, harmonized with bright green, neutral green, emerald green, cobalt blue, ultramarine blue and violet. Painting with a range of cold colours does not mean excluding from your palette reds, yellow and ochres; these can participate in harmonizing the picture as long as it offers a bluish trend.

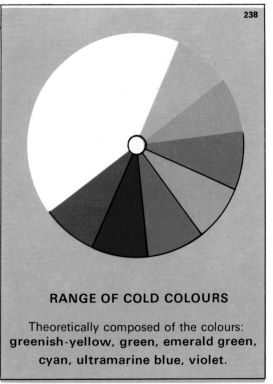

RANGE OF COLD COLOURS

Theoretically composed of the colours:
greenish-yellow, green, emerald green, cyan, ultramarine blue, violet.

The colours set out in this chart are the ones that, in theory, make up the range of cold colours. But in practice, the colours in this range are conditioned by those which the artist normally uses and which appear on this palette (fig. 237); that is (following the order of the palette, from bottom to top and from left to right):

Prussian blue, dark ultramarine blue, dark cobalt blue, emerald green, permanent green, deep madder, raw umber, yellow ochre.

Now study this magnificient portrait by Degás (fig. 239), so that you can understand too, that a range called *cold*, does not necessarily have to be blue... even when as a whole —even in the tendency of the flesh colours— it is blue.

Fig. 239.— Edgar Degás. "Portrait of a young woman". Louvre Museum, Paris. This is a good example of what was said at the end of the previous figure. This excellent portrait by Degás, uses harmonization of cold colours, not just because of the background blue nor the bluish black of the dress, but also because there's blue in the hair, in the shadows of the face and even in the flesh colour there's a hint of blue.

range of broken colours

240

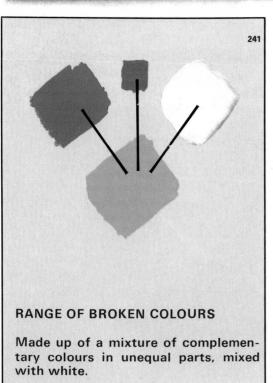

241

RANGE OF BROKEN COLOURS

Made up of a mixture of complementary colours in unequal parts, mixed with white.

Take two colours that complement each other, for example, green and intense red mix one part of green with a quarter of intense red and add as much white as you like. You will get a brown, khaki, ochre or green colour... which in any case will be greyish, "dirty"; darker, when the amount of one colour in comparison to the other is more similar, more greyish, according to how much white is added.

The picture reproduced on the following page (fig. 242) is a clear example of a picture resolved with a *range of broken colours*. You yourself can see the range of neutral, grey, "dirty" colours, dictated by the model itself, on a cloudy day, in an industrial theme with tenements, houses and buildings tainted by the soot from the engines.

Observe, moreover, that within this beautiful range of colours, broken, you can choose a cold or warm tendency. And lastly, see that the range of such colours does not exclude any colour from the palette.

Fig. 240.— All the colours of the palette may play a part in a range of broken colours, as long as they are not lively colours, raw colours, and are broken, dirty colours.

242

Fig. 242.— J. M. Parramón. "The bridge in Marina street". Private collection. A grey day and a grey theme, carriages and engines, smoke, soot, undefined colours, broken colours. A theme which nature set out like this and which I had the luck to see and paint. Observe that there are many different colours and tones, but that none of them stands out, except this crimson red in the centre carriage, from the railway, in which there still is, however, the mixture which converts it into a broken crimson, so that it harmonized with the whole. Choose a grey model, a grey day and try painting with a range of broken colours. It is, I believe sheer poetry.

the colour of flesh

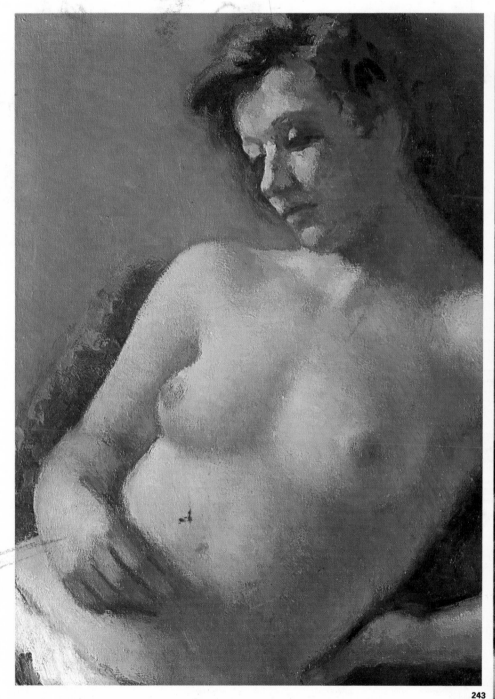

243

The famous painter Eugene Delacroix said on one occasion, "Give me mud and I will paint the skin of a Venus... on condition that I can paint around her, as the background, the colours that I want to."

Delacroix's sentence confirms the idea that there is no determinate flesh colour, that flesh colour depends on the background, on the form of lighting, that is, on the colour of the light, the intensity, the quality, the atmospheric reflections. And lastly, on the range the painter prefers. Francesc Serra, an excellent figure and female nude painter, once explained to me the composition of flesh colour. "Let me assure you that it is the same as or very similar to that used by Dutch artists in the XVIII century", he said. Here you have it in figure 245.

Fig. 243.— Francesc Serra "Nude". Private collection.

Fig. 244.— Velázquez "The Venus in the mirror". National Gallery, London.

Fig. 245.— The colour of flesh depends on many factors. See on the right the formula used by Francesc Serra, a specialist in nudes.

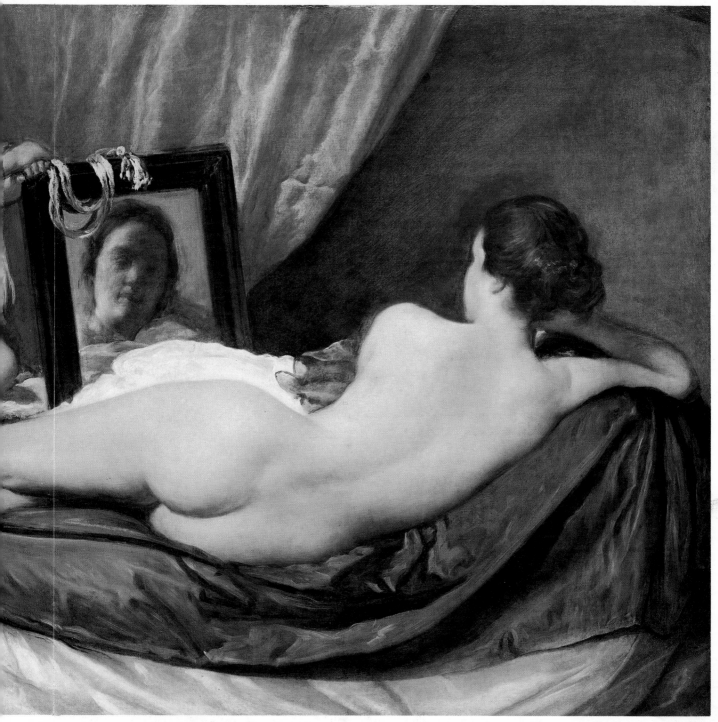

244

245

WHITE, mixed with **OCHRE** and with **ENGLISH RED**, gives a light flesh colour. Adding ultramarine blue it gives a dark flesh colour.

contrast of tone and colour

Curious, educational and practical is this question of contrasts.

The most well known effect is the one in figure 247, called *simultaneous contrast*. The rule about this says: *a colour is darker when the colour around it is lighter and, vice versa, a colour is lighter when the colour around it is darker*. Also within the field of *simultaneous contrasts* another well known one is that *the juxtaposition of the same colour in different tones, causes an apparent change of both tones with the light one becoming lighter and the dark one becoming darker* (Fig. 246).

Another effect to be taken into account is that of the *maximum contrast,* caused by the juxtaposition of two colours that are complementary to each other (Figs. 248 A, B, C, D, E, and F).

It is curious and serves for some cases, but not all, the so-called *induction of complementary colours,* which can be explained by saying: *in order to modify a certain colour it is enough to change the colour of the background surrounding it* (Fig. 249). The green square looks blue on a yellow background and yellower on a blue background).

Lastly, let's play at *the phenomenon of successive images*. Look steadily at the three coloured balloons on a white background in figure 250, concentrating your eyes on the centre of the picture, that is on the red balloon, for about thirty seconds in a very

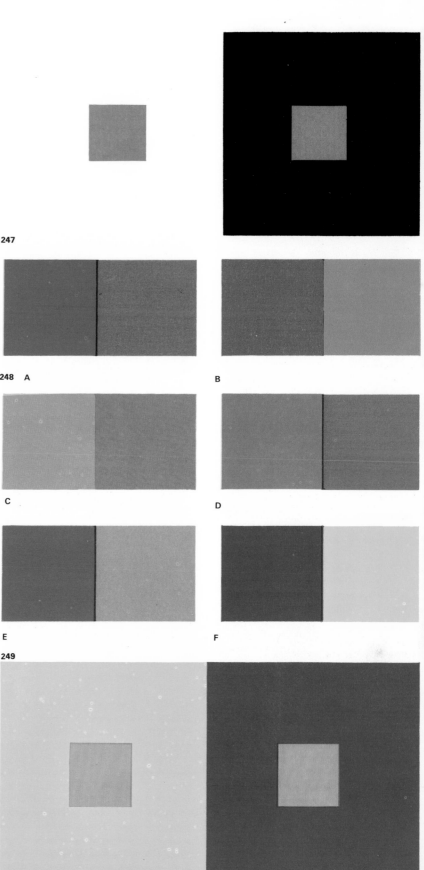

247

248 A

B

C

D

E

F

249

246

Fig. 246.— The juxtaposition of two different colours, causes the enhancement of both, lightening the light one and darkening the dark one. Looked at separately, each of these strips is regular in tone, without variation, but looked at one on above the other we can observe a considerable variation in tones, and each strip is lighter at the top edge and darker at the lower edge.

Fig. 247.— (left). Because of the law of simultaneous contrasts, the purple square printed on a white background, seems darker than the same purple square on a black background.

Fig. 248.— The maximum contrast given by one colour (independently of its tone) is the one offered by the juxtaposition of two complementary colours. The use of these juxtapositions may cause effects of great artistic quality in some compositions. It can also be the cause of unpleasant dissonances, as occurs, for example, in pictures 248 A and B.

Fig. 249.— The "sympathy" of complementary colours, Chevreul's law, according to which *a colour casts over the neighbouring shade its own complementary colour,* is obvious in this illustration, in which the green square on a yellow background, has a slight bluish tendency, while the green square on a blue background shows a slight yellowish tendency.

Fig. 250.— The physicist Chevreul established "the vision of any colour at all created by "sympathy" the appearance of the complementary one". This law may be tested here and now by you yourself, looking steadily for half a minute with a good light, at the balloons printed on a white background on this page.

After thirty seconds, move your eyes little higher, on the same white background and you will see the same forms, the same balloons, in their complementary colours.

250

well-lit room. Then lift your eyes a little higher, to the centre of the white space, and you will see on the white paper, relatively clearly, the three balloons in their complementary colours, that is, the yellow one blue, the red one cyan, and the blue one yellow. The colours of such after images are very pale.

The *induction of complementary colours* and the *phenomenon of successive images* lead us to the evidence that the vision of any colour whatsoever creates, by "sympathy", the appearance of the complementary colour. The physicist, Chevreul, classified these phenomena with this rule:

a colour casts over its neighbouring shade its own complementary colour contrasts of tone and colour

contrast of tone and colour

Fig. 251.— Francesc Serra. "Reading", private collection. In this picture the artist took into account *the induction of complementary colours,* painting a grey, greenish, yellowish face, but on a blue background, which by induction adds red (the complement of blue) to the colour painted on the face.

Fig. 252.— Paul Cézanne. "The card players". Impressionist Museum. Paris. Observe the *simultaneous contrasts* provoked by Cézanne in this work, analyzing the backgrounds and surroundings where the artist darkens or lightens as necessary, so that the forms have more relief, are more visible, and are better delineated.

Simultaneous contrasts, maximum contrasts, induction of complementary colours, successive images... What's the use of all this? We are going to look at it from a practical point of view:

If you want to modernize your themes and your palette, remember the contrast of colour provoked by two juxtaposed complementary hues, one touching the other. Try to find these effects even before painting, when you analyze or compose the subject. Think of the possibility of changing colours.

If you want an object to stand out from the background, and take on relief, offer a more lively surround, provoke a simultaneous contrast between the outline and the background, between the brightness of the object and the darker tone of the background, or vice versa. In this connection, look at what Cézanne used to do —what we all do— in *The card players,* in figure 252. Observe the colours, false and dark, painted behind (in the background) the heads, the arms, to give emphasis to the figures.

Bear in mind the *induction of complementary colours* and the phenomenon *of the successive images* by always painting first the background and then the subject placed in front, in order to be able to adjust and harmonize colours. Try to paint *at the same time, all at the same time,* filling the whole canvas, leaving no white areas, remembering especially Chevreul's definitive sentence:

Putting a brush stroke of colour on a canvas is not just staining the canvas with the colour on the brush. It is too, colouring the space around it with its conplementary colour.

technique and skill of oil painting

learn to see and mix colours

Technique and skill. Both can be learnt. Knowing how to see and mix colours, for example. Something that one learns seeing, imagining, trying and finally painting.

Let us try out this process now:

Look at figure 253. This range of colours, ochre, red, purples, violets and mulberries, was printed with only three colours, yellow, magenta and cyan as you can see in the three samples of colour printed in a smaller size. Have you seen it? Well, it's a question of covering with a piece of paper the three samples at the bottom and choosing any colour at all from figure 253, and imagining how much yellow, magenta and cyan are needed to make it up. Example; the colour F (the mulberry in the middle) —what colour is it? Imagine the colour and then look at the solution: 0% yellow, 90% magenta and 20% cyan. What colour is it? Ask yourself this question at any time, at home, looking at the colour of an orange —...cadmium red, cadmium yellow and a little crimson—, looking at the colour of an unvarnished piece of furniture —...ochre, white, maybe a little ultramarine blue. Look at the sky and ask yourself what colour it is, imagining that there is blue, white, more white then blue, and a touch of crimson.

Then when you have the subject in front of you, the exercise will be the same, but with a lot more possibilities of being right.

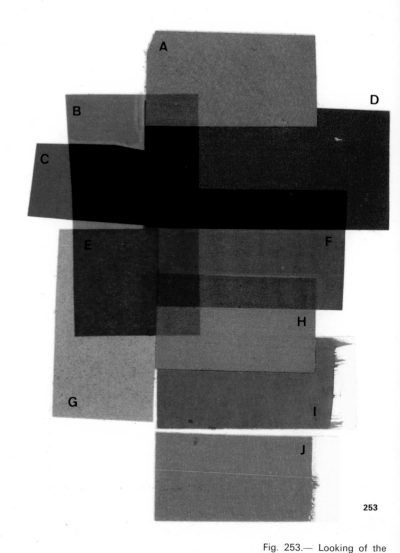

253

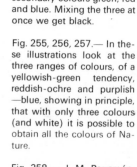

Fig. 253.— Looking of the colours that appear in this figure, and selecting one of them, try to analyze and judge the colours you would have to mix, and in what proportion, to make up the selected colour.

Fig. 254.— (Above right). Mixing the three primary colours in pairs we obtain the secondary colours green, red and blue. Mixing the three at once we get black.

Fig. 255, 256, 257.— In these illustrations look at the three ranges of colours, of a yellowish-green tendency, reddish-ochre and purplish —blue, showing in principle, that with only three colours (and white) it is possible to obtain all the colours of Nature.

Fig. 258.— J. M. Parramón. "Landscape of the Catalan Pyrenees". Private collection. Painted with three colours and white.

mixture of three colours and white

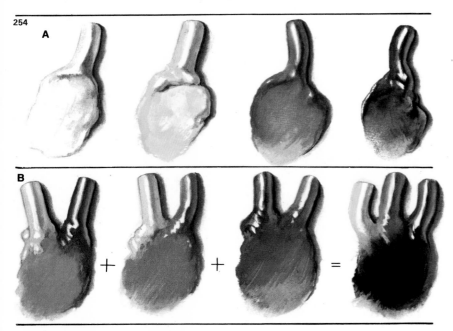

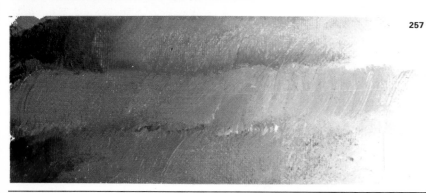

The first practical exercise that anyone who wants to learn to paint hundreds of different colours by mixing a few should undertake is that of painting with only three colours and white.

Three basic colours that cannot be made up with any other: yellow, magenta and cyan. As you will have guessed these are the three *primary colours,* on the basis of which, mixing some with others (with the help of white whenever necessary), you can make up all the colours of Nature.

When painting in oils the three above mentioned colours are:

1. *Medium cadmium yellow.*
2. *Deep madder*
3. *Prussian blue.*

See in figures 254 A and 254 B, how to obtain the three *secondary colours,* green, red and blue, by mixing the primary colours in pairs. Observe that mixing the three primary colours gives black.

Likewise study the ranges of colour reproduced in figures 255, 256 and 257, achieved with the yellow, magenta and cyan mentioned above. Lastly, look at this landscape painted with only the three colours mentioned and white. Incredible? We are going to do it together, starting on the following page.

composition of warm colours

COLOURS OF WALLS WITH SUN

1   2   3   4   5

COLOURS OF WALLS IN SHADOW

6   7   8   9

VARIOUS COLOURS

11   12   13   14   15   259

To work! Let's paint! First as an experiment, practising the art of seeing and mixing colours, then we'll paint a coloured sketch which you will feel proud of.

Let's get down to it: imagine you are painting an urban landscape: the one in figure number 260. It's five o'clock in the afternoon: the sunlight, with the sun going down, colours the old walls of this old square, golden, yellow, ochre, orangey colours; in the shadowed parts, all the surfaces and all the bodies run with vermilion, red.

You are going to compose these colours —I beg you to do it—, painting just with the three primary colours.

REQUIRED MATERIALS:

Oil colours: cadmium yellow medium; deep madder; Prussian blue.
Canvas, or cardboard, or heavy paper.
Brushes: 5 flat number 8 or 10 hogs' hair brushes.
Other: palette, turpentine, cloths, pieces of newspaper.

1. - More luminous walls. Mix yellow with white and add a little crimson.

2. - More luminous walls. Add a little more yellow to the previous colour, plus a touch more crimson.

3. - General colour. (Clean the brush), take yellow and add a little white and crimson.

4. - Dark luminous colour: only yellow and a little crimson, there's no white.

5. - Walls on the left: add crimson and a little white to the previous colour.

6. - Lighter walls in shadow. (Clean the brush or change it for a clean one). Yellow and crimson, with almost no white, and a little of blue.

7. - Turret shadows. Begin with yellow and gradually add crimson. Without white, without blue.

8. - More Intense shadows. The previous colour with crimson added.

9. - Darker shadows. The same previous colour, with a little more yellow, adding crimson and a little blue.

10. - Black in the shadows. Deep madder and a little blue. Try to get a warm black.

11. - Greenish ochre. Yellow, white and a little crimson, add blue progressively (Careful with Prussian blue! It's very strong).

12. - Vermilion lighten a little crimson with white and add yellow (but as you can see, it's not a brilliant red. This is one of the few colours that is not obtained with only the three primary colours).

13. - Warm purple. Made up of crimson and white, adding a little yellow.

14. - Dark sap green. Begin by making up a medium brilliant green, with yellow and blue. Then add crimson until you get this dirty green.

15. - Black with a greenish tendency. The same colour as before, adding more blue and crimson.

260

Fig. 260.— J. M. Parramón. "Plaza Nueva, fiesta de San Roc". Private collection. Example of harmonizing of warm colours.

composition of warm colours

WARM FLESH COLOURS

16   17   18   19   20

WARM GREENS

21   22   23   24   25

WARM GREYS BLUES

26   27   28   29   30

261

We are still painting with three colours, but this time we are not conditioned by a definite model. We are going to paint three series of warm colours, the first of flesh colours, the second of warm greens and the last of warm greys and blues.

The same colours. White, cadmium yellow medium, deep madder and Prussian blue, and the same materials.

16. - *Luminous flesh colour*. A lot of white, a little yellow and a little crimson.

17. - *Pinkish flesh colour*. The previous colour with a little more yellow and a touch more crimson.

18. - *Yellow ochre*. Yellow and white in almost equal amounts, a little crimson and a little blue.

19. - *Raw Sienna*. The previous colour adding more crimson, more yellow and a little more blue.

20. - *English red*. Crimson and white until you get this tone, then add a little yellow.

21. - *Yellow green*. (Clean the brushes, please). Yellow and white, then add blue gradually until you get this tone. Lastly a little crimson to "dirty" the green.

22. - *Light green*. The previous colour with a little more blue.

23. - *Bright green*. Yellow and blue (with no white) and a little crimson to make the colour warmer.

24. - *Warm dark green*. The previous colour with blue, added gradually, until you get this intensity.

25. - *Black with a greenish tendency*. The previous colour with more blue and red.

26. - *Warm grey*. White, blue and crimson to get a very light purple, then add yellow gradually, until you reach this colour.

27. - *Warm bluish grey*. To the previous colour add a very small amount of blue and crimson.

28. - *Warm neutral grey*. To the previous colour add a little yellow, blue and crimson.

29. - *Warm bluish grey*. (Better clean the brush). A little white, a little more blue and crimson until you get a bluish mulberry, which can then be made greyer with a little yellow.

30. - *Dark grey blue*. To the previous colour, add blue and a little crimson.

composition of cold colours

COLD
FLESH
COLOURS

31   32   33   34   35

COLD
GREEN
COLOURS

36   37   38   39   40

GREYISH
BLUE
COLOURS

41   42   43   44   45

262

As on the previous page, but now working with a range of cold colours, we are going to paint three series of colours, the first of flesh colours, another of greens and the last of greys and blues.

Materials the same as in the previous sessions.

I advise you to begin with clean palette and brushes.

31. - Flesh colour shining parts. White and insignificant amounts of yellow, crimson and blue in similar proportions, emphasizing the crimson.

32. - Cold flesh colour. White, a little yellow, a little crimson, until you get a pale orange, then you must gradually add blue until you get this tone.

34. - Flesh colour in shadows. White, yellow and blue, until you get a light green, then gradually add yellow and crimson.

35. - Flesh colour in shadow. With crimson, blue and a little white, make up a purple with a reddish tendency, add a little yellow and on the basis of this Sienna colour, add white and blue.

36. - Light blue. White, a little blue and a little yellow.

37. - Bluish green. The same as before with a little more blue.

38. - Bright green. Yellow and blue. No crimson, no white.

39. - Dark permanent green. The sa-

me as before with more blue.

40. - Dark green. Add more blue and a small amount of crimson to the previous colour.

41. - Light blue-grey. (Clean the brushes, please). White and blue until you have a pale blue, then add a very small amount of crimson and the same of yellow.

42. - Medium blue-grey. The same as before, increasing the proportion of blue.

43. - Cold Blue-Grey. The same as before, increasing the blue and slightly the crimson.

44. — Blue violet. Add a little crimson to the previous colour number 42.

45. - Intense blue-grey. The same as before adding blue and a little of yellow.

127

composition of cold colours

COLOURS OF THE EARTH AND AWNINGS

46 47 48 49 50

COLOURS OF THE SKY AND THE SEA

51 52 53 54 55

BLUE SHADOWS DOORS SIENNAS

56 57 58 59 60

263

Now we are going to paint a range of cold colours, corresponding to the picture on the following page, a seascape where greens and blues predominate (figure 264). We are still using the same materials.

46. - Colour of the earth with light. A lot of white with a little yellow and a touch of crimson, and you get a cream colour which has to be "dirtied" with a little blue.

47. - Normal earth colour. The previous colour adding yellow, crimson and a little blue.

48. - Earth colour in the background mountains. White, blue and crimson, until you get a warm purple, then add yellow and blue until you get this colour.

49. - Awning on the left. The previous colour with a little blue and a small amount of yellow.

50. - Awning on the right. the previous colour with a little blue and a small amount of yellow.

51. - Shining parts of the water. (Clean or change brushes). White and a little Prussian blue.

52. — Shining parts of the water. The previous colour with a little more blue and a little bit of yellow.

53. - Colour of the water. (left). The same as before, with more blue and a small amount of crimson, but there isn't any yellow.

54. - Colour of the water in general and part of the sky. The previous colour with more blue and a little crimson.

55. - Colour of the sky. The previous colour with more blue and a little yellow.

56. - Blue-grey shadows. White, blue, a little crimson, very little until you get a luminous blue. Then add a little yellow to "dirty" it.

57. - Blue shadows. Lighten the previous colour with white and then add a little blue.

58. - The green of the doors on the right. Add yellow to the previous colour, then mix with a little crimson to make it greyer.

59. - Dark Siennas reflected in the water. Crimson and yellow making up an English red, then add blue, gradually until you get this burnt umber colour.

60. - Cold black inside the houses. Prussian blue and a little crimson.

264

Fig. 264.— J. M. Parramón. "Fornells". Private collection. Example of harmonizing cold colours.

composition of broken colours

SKY;
MOUNTAINS,
AND
FIELDS

COLOURS
OF THE
HOUSES

Imagine you are painting a country-side completed with a range of broken colours like the one you can see on the following page (figure 266). Here we have then, how to obtain this extensive range of colours, tones and shades, with the mixture of only three colours, yellow, crimson and blue, as well as white.

61. - Colour of the sky. (Clean the brushes). A lot of white, a little blue until you get a light sky blue, and then continue with a little crimson and a little less yellow.

62. - Colour of the mountains. Blue, a little white and crimson.

63. - Green of the field in general. First make a brilliant green with blue and yellow, them make it greyer with white.

64. - Dark green of the field. The same colour as before adding blue and crimson.

65. - Green of the field in the middle. The same green as before adding white, crimson and yellow.

66. - Grey house in left foreground. White, blue and crimson, until you get a bluish brown, then add yellow until you get this grey.

67. - Colour of the shadow of the same house. The same colour increasing the proportions of the previous mixture.

68. - House in the background, on the left. First make up a light green with white, yellow and blue, then pro-gressively add a little crimson and yellow.

69. - Reddish house in the background. White, yellow and crimson, to get a light orange with a reddish tendency, then add a little blue.

70. - Shadow of the same reddish house. The same colour adding blue and crimson.

71. - Colour of the path crossing the centre. White, yellow, a little crimson and even less blue.

72. - Light grey wall with gate, in the centre. White, blue, a little crimson and less yellow.

73. - Greys in forms near the wall in the foreground. The previous colour adding the same colours in proportion.

74. - The colour of the walls. The same colour as before increasing the proportions of each colour.

75. - Colour of the tree trunks. Crimson and blue and a little yellow to get the warm broken colour.

266

Fig. 266.— J. M. Parramón. "Landscape in the Catalan Pyrenees". Private collection. Example of a theme painted with a range of broken colours.

composition of broken colours

VARIOUS COLOURS

OCHRES AND BROKEN SIENNAS

VARIOUS BROKEN COLOURS

Here we have a last range of broken colours where, without the conditioning of a certain scene, I have composed a series of shades and neutral colours, which are neither warm nor cold, that is to say, they are broken.

76. - Greyish ivory colour. (Remember, palette and brushes clean). First make up a rosy cream colour and then add a little blue.

77. - Greyish ochre. The previous colours, increasing the proportions.

78. - Greyish purple. The same as the previous colour adding crimson and a little blue.

79. - Natural umber. The same colour as before adding yellow and blue.

80. - Dark purple. The same colour as before, adding blue and a little crimson.

81. - Light ochre. (Clean brushes). White, yellow, a little crimson and a little blue.

82. - Dark yellow ochre. The same as the previous one, slightly increasing the proportions, and adding a little more crimson.

83. - Burnt Sienna. White, yellow and crimson, until you get a reddish orange, then add a very little blue.

84. - Burnt umber. Add to the previous one, crimson and a little blue.

85. - Dark raw umber. First compose a dark purple with blue, crimson and a little white, then add yellow and more white if necessary.

86. - Spoiled white. (Clean the brushes). White, crimson and yellow, in small amounts, then add very small doses of blue until you get this colour.

87. - Light, yellowish green. The previous colour adding a little yellow and blue.

88. - Greyish light green. The previous colour adding a little yellow, less blue and even less crimson.

89. - Bluish grey. (Clean brushes). Compose a sky blue, with white and blue and then add a small amount of yellow and crimson.

90. - Bluish grey medium. The same colour as before, adding blue, a little crimson and a very little yellow.

painting with three colours and white

If you are a professional painter skip over this page and the four following ones. If you are an amateur with some experience, stop, read and look at what is said and illustrated on these pages and consider the possibility of doing this exercise which, as you will see, could be good "gymnastics" for you. If you are an amateur who has never, or almost never, painted in oils, you must do this exercise. When you have finished you will be surprised at your ability to paint pictures.

In the adjoining photograph you can see the model for the picture you are going to paint (figure 268). It is a simple still life, placed on a corner of a table, covered with a white cloth, made up of a plain clay vase, a dark green pottery dish, with four or five pieces of fruit, two oranges, a peach and a lemon a bunch of grapes, a glass with a little wine in it and an apple. In the background looms the back of a chair against a uniform grey wall. The illumination is against the light, that is to say, with the light coming from behind the subject. It is important to note, lastly, that to soften the contrast of this lighting effect, with the help of two chairs. I installed two white canvases, one on each side and in front of the subject, which as reflecting screens, to a certain extent compensated for the excessive contrast, the drama of the illumination against the light. In the adjoining figure 269 you can see what I did to improve the illumination of the model. Let me say, lastly, that the important thing in this exercise is not exactly the subject or the fact of painting from the natural, although the latter can always be recommended, but rather the experience of painting a picture with all the colours presented by the subject, using only the three primary colours, cyan, magenta and yellow, as well as white. If you paint this picture with these three colours, *even copying it from what I myself have painted* which appears on the page 137, I assure you that you will paint better from now on, because you really have pracrised the composition and mixture of colours.

In the adjoining chart you can see the materials required to carry out this exercise.

268

Fig. 268.— This is the subject I prepared in order to paint a picture with three colours and white. The background corresponds to a white wall in shadow. The light comes from behind the subject.

269

Fig. 269.— A picture against the light offers a luminous rim on the upper outlines of the objects and the rest remains in shadow. It generally turns out to be a subject with not much colour, and a lot of contrast. To soften this excessive contrast I placed two large canvas reflecting screens which allowed me to paint with more light, with more colour. In this picture you can see the location of the window where light enters the studio, which I placed much lower, so that it would appear in the picture.

MATERIALS REQUIRED TO CARRY OUT THIS EXERCIXE

Charcoal	1 hog's hair brush no. 4
Spray for fixing charcoal	2 hog's hair brushed no. 6
Cardboard-canvas n.º 3.	2 hog's hair brushes no. 8
Figure	3 hog's hair brushes no. 10
Oil colours:	2 hog's hair brushes no. 12
Cadmium yellow medium	1 spatula in form of trowel
Deep madder	1 oil dipper
Prussian blue	1 small container for
Titian white	turpentine.
Palette	

how to begin a picture

Before starting to paint it's natural for the artist, to contemplate the subject for a while, considering the light and shade effects, studying the contrast, analyzing forms and colours, trying to imagine what the finished picture will look like, and in this way the artist enters the field of interpretation, imagines and mentally changes forms, contrasts and colours.

I myself, before beginning to paint, made this analysis of the model. "I don't like such a regular background. As there is, higher up in this wall, a large window, I'll paint this window lower down to break the monotony of the background."

"I don't like the grapes, they're old and ugly. I'll paint fresh grapes from memory".

"I don't like the apple, it lacks colour; I'll paint it with reds as well as yellows."

"In the tablecloth, in the foreground, I'll paint some grey-ochre cream wrinkles..."

This series of reflections is usually made concrete in a preliminary sketch but we'll do without this previous study and pass directly to beginning the picture.

But how do we begin the picture? By first drawing the model? By painting directly, without a previous drawing? Here we have an old controversy. It is possible to say that those artists who paint with hardly any shadows, illuminating the bodies with frontal or diffuse light, seeing and differentiating objects with stains of colour (Van Gogh, Matisse, Bonard, etc.), that is to say, the "colourists", usually begin the picture directly, while those who paint with light and shadows (Chardin, Corot —Corot said to Pisarro: "Start by drawing the shadows"—, Manet, Nonell, Dalí, etc.) who could be called "judgers", generally begin the picture by drawing the model. But let's say that between the two extremes, there is an intermediate general plan which consists of drawing a fast sketch, to orientate yourself. See, as an example of this synthesis of construction, the drawing in figure 270.

But we are going to draw the theme with some precision, making sure of the dimensions and proportions, the overall effect so that then we can paint with more assurance.

This is the charcoal drawing that I did as the previous step to beginning to paint (figure 271). Once the drawing is finished it has to be fixed.

Fig. 270.— Hand-raised sketch, with which the professional usually begins an oil picture. It was done with a number 4 round hog's hair brush, and with Prussian blue and burnt umber, mixed with turpentine.

270

Fig. 271.— To ensure the construction and to make a previous study of the evaluation of the picture, some professionals draw the model in charcoal with a few touches of rubber eraser to clean the white parts. A drawing of this kind has to be fixed.

271

where to begin painting - first stage

The *law of simultaneous contrasts* —you remember— tells us that a colour is lighter or darker according to the background colour that surrounds it. Keeping this rule in mind, it would be a mistake to begin to paint, on the white of the canvas, with a small area or isolated object, giving it a value that could become lighter or darker, according to the colour of the background we are going to paint afterwards.

Consequently we have to paint the large white spaces. As soon as possible, we have to begin with the biggest areas. In this picture we will begin with the bluish-grey background and we will carry on with the luminous colours of the large window, then the clay vase, the fruit...

Generally speaking, I paint ignoring some parts of the drawing, like the outlines of the handles on the vase, the back of the chair.

I paint the outside light of the windows, and then I change the brush for a clean one.

Be careful when changing brushes. Never try to paint a light colour using a brush on which there are still traces of a dark colour. It is essential to clean them from time to time.

Be careful with the grapes. They always present a drawing problem, easy to deal with if you are careful to draw them exactly and correctly. You have to count the grapes, watch their size, their positions within the bunch, and the shapes of the dark holes between grape and grape.

I put colour on the apple in the foreground and on the wine in the glass.

I go on with a few cream-coloured stains in the foreground of the tablecloth, which later on I will use as the shadows of creases.

And I leave it (figure 272).

I take a short rest. It is time to smoke a cigarette or drink a glass of something, time to reconsider, to study...

I clean the brushes, I clean the palette.

Fig. 272.— In this first stage we only lightly stain the canvas in order to be better able, from now on, to adjust the colour and the contrast of some elements in relation to others.

272

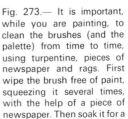

273

Fig. 273.— It is important, while you are painting, to clean the brushes (and the palette) from time to time, using turpentine, pieces of newspaper and rags. First wipe the brush free of paint, squeezing it several times, with the help of a piece of newspaper. Then soak it for a few minutes in a small container of turpentine, and rinse and squeeze the brush again, but now with a rag which, after repeating the operation two or three times, leaves the brush practically clean.

second stage

Fig. 274. — In this second stage there is a colouring and a contrast that are more appropriate to the subject, but still shaping, in large washes, in practically flat colours, the forms and colours of the elements that make up the picture. It is a stage close to the final one, but in synthesis, a synthesis which allows us to see the possibilities of developing towards a final version which we can forsee as correct.

274

I begin with the tablecloth. As well as blue and white I see that I'll have to add a few touches of this cream colour I painted in the foreground. I paint the illuminated surround of the fruit with light blue and a little crimson. I take advantage of this purple to stain the reflection of the wine in the glass.

Now I paint the illuminated outline or the apple in the foreground and go on to repaint the vase.

I have darkened the background but I think I've gone too far. I have worked for a while on the bluish lights around the vase... I paint the chair. I paint the dish. It is very dark in the subject and I decide to paint it lighter. I paint the apple in the foreground, the shadows of the dish on the tablecloth, and the shadows of the apple, the grapes, the glass... I finish the apple in the foreground... and I am going to repaint the fruit in the dish. Which I do with clean, bright colours...

I leave it like this, as you can see in this figure 274.

last stage

Fig. 275.— And in fact, starting from the previous synthesis it was relatively easy to reach this ending where, apart from adjusting colours and contrasts —that of the window in the background and the background itself, making them lighter. The reflections of light on the vase and the fruit were made less blue and the general colour of the tablecloth whiter. I worried specially about diversifying the colour and creating and accentuating this atmosphere and this "celestial light", that is spiritual, lyrical, and poper and exclusive to illumination against the light.

275

As you can see, in this last session —three days after the previous one—, I "repented" of many forms and colours, and I painted and repainted, always with colours and white, until I had retouched all the colours of the picture.

Look and compare. In this final version everything is less blue, the background is lighter, the tablecloth whiter, the vase more luminous, less dirty (how I suffered with that vase, doing and redoing it...!). In the end I think, that in this final condition the picture has more atmosphere, more realism, thanks to the fact that the forms and the shadows are less concrete, more ethereal, presenting better an effect of instantaneous impression. Observe and compare, for example, the shadows projected onto the tablecloth from the dish of fruit, the bunch of grapes, the glass, the apple...

And note. with only three colours and white.

two and half hours to paint a picture

276

Fig. 276.— This is the model that I selected to paint and explain the technique of direct painting. A view of the village named Torla, in the Aragonese Pyrenees, a few kilometres from the French frontier.

Fig. 277.— With a round hogs hair brush, lightly-loaded with colour (Prussian blue and burnt umber), and soaked in turpentine, as if I were painting in water colours, here we have a rapid sketch —not more than a quarter of an hour— in which, by synthesizing the complexity of the model, the main elements are placed and I am ready to start painting.

277

The impressionists were the ones who introduced *the technique of direct painting*. They painted their landscapes in a single session and they took only three or four hours to begin and finish a picture. They tried to capture the impression of the moment and they managed to do it! How? By painting *directly*.

> *By painting from the first moment with the same form as the definitive resolution.*

This to a great extent depends on the experience and craft one has, but which is also subject to the artist's attitude to the picture.

The normal situation is that you and I and everyone who paints, never, or almost never, make use of all our intellectual capacity. It's common to work without concentrating completely because, we know the "there's always a second time", a second or third session to redo it, regret, rectify, but with the formula invented by the Impressionists of "one picture, one session", there's no second time! The artist has to think that there's only one opportunity to complete the picture, the form, the colour, and he has to discipline himself not to go back over what he's done, to finish it "alla prima", at the first try. He has to feel compromised from the beginning to the end of the picture.

It's a *question of attitude*. But there is too, a technical process that you can follow in these pictures and text.

Fig. 278.— The initial drawing is still there. Now it's a question of filling in spaces with different shades of green, with ochres and Siennas dictated by the scene, but without absolute subjection to it. Follow too your aesthetic sense, the composition and understanding, the forms and the harmonization of the colours in general.

278

279

Fig. 279.— Paint which is thicker but not much. Resolution of the picture I first intended, with a second layer, painting as they say from the top to the bottom, following the model but interpreting, synthesizing, simplifying forms and colours, fields, trees and bushes. And especially, I would almost say **above all** DIVERSIFYING the colour. Total time for finishing the picture, two and a half hours.

painting in several sessions

Trying to define this technique we would say that: *it's the one that resolves the picture in several sessions, with the paint dry or semi dry, refining the drawing, the modelling, the contrast and the colouring.*

It is the technique of the old masters still put into practice by many artists, specially in *easel pictures,* that is to say, in pictures painted in the studio such as still lifes, portraits and figures in general, relatively large in size.

From the beginning, the technique to be followed is completely different from that of direct painting. In painting by stages, first we have the worry of drawing and modelling —shadowing, illuminating—, leaving the colouring for later.

The first part, in which the artist draws and models, begins with thin layers of almost monochrome paint, with influences of warm or cold colours, according to the range of harmonization worked out beforehand.

On this solid initial basis, we then begin applying the real colour in thicker layers, allowing painting and repainting, with its consequent rubbings and scrubbings.

As an example of this technique see the nude reproduced on this page, painted in oil by Francesc Serra. (figures 280 to 283).

Francesc Serra painted this picture on a number 40, figure canvas. First he drew several studies in charcoal to decide on the model's pose. He began the picture with a charcoal drawing and completed the first painting session with a very limited palette, painting with only five basic colours, silver white, black, burnt sienna, yellow ochre and burnt umber, a very neutral range of colours that is greyish and rather dirty, as you can see in the fragment reproduced in figure 280. Observe in this reproduction the remains of the charcoal lines that draw the model.

280

281

282

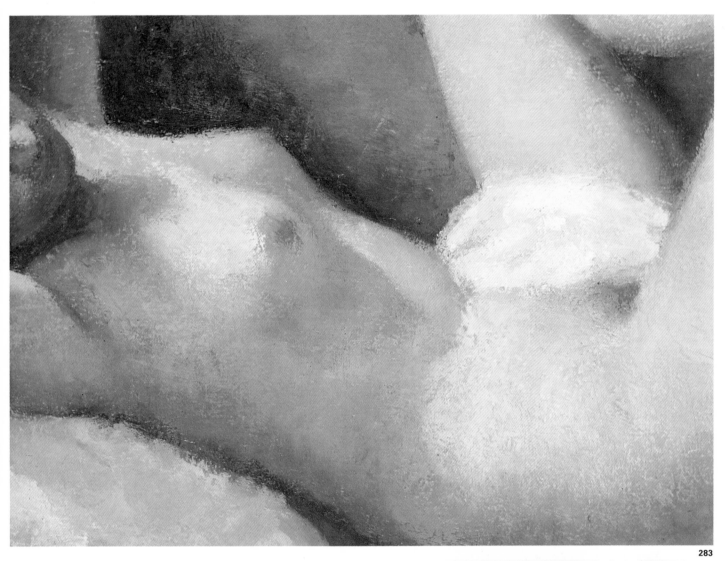

283

Five days later, Serra returned to the picture with the idea of *painting*, with the intention too of elaborating the material, of enriching the dough. Serra, like many artists, was working on five or six pictures at the same time. He would leave them and take them up again three or four days later, working no more than two hours at each session (fig. 281).

Lastly see the finished picture, which was reached after three more sessions, during which he increased and intensified the colour, studied and calculated slight changes working with more and more material, applying more and more the technique of frottis as can be seen in the enlarged reproduction of fig. 283.

Francesc Serra died a few years ago. I was lucky enough to be with him, in his studio in Tossa de Mar, while he painted this picture. Francesc Serra liked Titian very much.

Fig. 283.— Francesc Serra. "Nude" (fragment). Private collection. As can be guessed from this reproduction, Francesc Serra liked painting with thick impastos, showing up the material, the way one layer was superimposed on another, and following to certain extent the techniques of *frottis* practised by Titian and Rembrandt (pages 28 and 36).

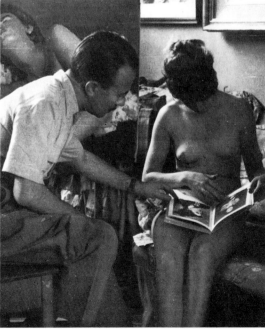

Fig. 284.— The artist Francesc Serra, talking with his model, in a few minutes rest, during one of his painting sessions.

284

technique and skill

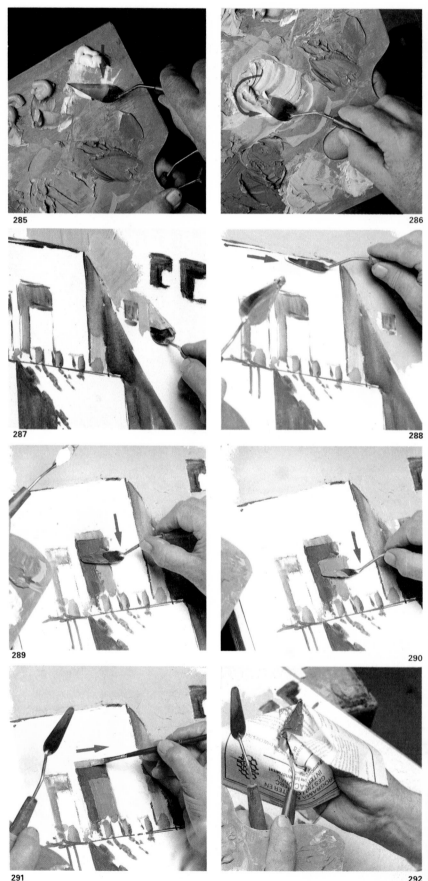

The technique of painting with a knife is somewhat complicated, necessitates skill, and is different, as we shall see:

In knife painting no solvents are used, the colours are mixed and applied thick, just as they come out of the tube. The palette is used in the same way to mix, collect and prepare colour, and one works with a maximum of three or four knives of different sizes but generally with the shape of a trowel.

When starting to paint you can do so with the knife, directly, or on top of a previous, very thin painting, done with brushes and colours diluted in abundant turpentine. The latter procedure allows the artist to have a background, which covers those parts, small areas or intersections, where the knife hasn't touched, given that "reaching" everywhere and, at the same time, constructing without undoing, presents its problems and difficulties. To achieve a more modern style, it is possible to mix and obtain shades and colours, on the canvas itself, without using the palette.

The very large areas are painted at the first try, in the first phase or condition, trying not to touch them or retouch them in the following phases. For the more broken up areas or parts, with more diverse, smaller and more complex shapes, it is advisable to apply colours that have already been mixed on the palette. In the last stage, in order to put the finishing touches, it is perfectly valid to touch up and repaint with a sable brush.

Painting a picture with a knife

Trying not to destroy the smooth, enamel

painting a picture with a knife

appearance, characteristic of oil painting by knife.

Lastly, I still have to say that knife painting can be completed with large impastos of colour, superimposing some on top of others, or with a practically normal thickness of paint that covers, however, the grain of the canvas. This technique, starting from a layer of thin paint, put on with a brush, was the one I used myself to paint with a knife the patio you can see in the picture that appears on this page and the following.

Fig. 285.—To take colour from the palette, the knife cuts off a part and scrapes it, taking it away.

Fig. 286.— Mixtures are made by crushing one colour with another and beating them both, moving the knife in a circular fashion.

Fig. 287.— Putting the colour on the canvas.

Fig. 288.— To draw a line or straight outline, load the back of the knife and apply it to the canvas, scraping the knife and applying the colour at the same time.

Fig. 289.— When painting a limit like the dark green shadow of the door, it is possible that with the spatula you go over the line. This is normal and is not important...

Fig. 290.— ...because it is also normal to superimpose colours in order to draw and reconstruct shapes.

Fig. 291.— The small shapes have to be painted with a sable hair brush.

Fig. 292.— The knife can be cleaned perfectly well with pieces of newspaper.

Fig. 293.— First stage of a picture painted with a knife, with a previous drawing painted in oil colour diluted in turpentine.

Fig. 294.— Second stage-painted with a brush, with very liquid paint.

Fig. 295.— Third stage, begin by painting the largest areas (in this case adjusting and changing colours). Note the reliefs caused by the knife.

293

294

295

Fig. 296.— Painting with a knife can produce workmanship of great impastos, where the paint reaches an obvious thickness. It can also be done with a half impasto, as in this picture, which covers the grain of the canvas and in the same way gives a finish that is typical of the knife. This seems to be the better formula, for pictures of rather smaller dimensions than this, where the painting has been done on a No. 8 Figure canvas (38 × 46 cm).

296

As you can see in this finished picture, the knife has resolved the form and colour of the walls and the doors and windows in general. In the latter, a sable hair brush played a part in painting and touching up small shapes like the bars on the lower window. The flower pots and the plants, together with their shadows, projected onto the front wall, were painted with sable brushes.

The sable hair brush should play only a minimal part, leaving the knife to construct the shapes and reflecting in the picture the difficulties of finish that this supposes, with which one obtains a "knife finish", that is to say, not very concrete, a little unsure, but really interesting and artistic.

you paint
in the same way
as you draw

Drawing makes up three quarters
of what painting is. If I had
to put a sign up over my door,
I would write: School of
Drawing, and I am sure it would
produce painters.

Jean-Auguste Dominique Ingres

construction

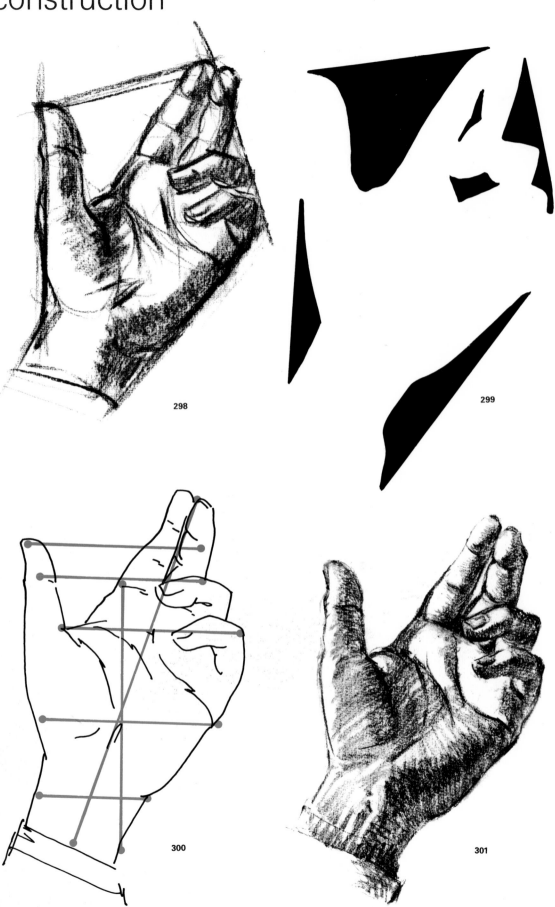

298

299

300

301

DRAWING AND CON-
STRUCTION OF YOUR
LEFT HAND

This is an exercise that I
invite you to try in order to
study and better understand
what form, volume, light and
shadow are and what tonal
evaluation is. You can carry
out this exercise on normal
drawing paper, with a soft
grade pencil, a 2B for example. Place your left hand
in this position or a similar
one and go.

Fig. 298.— Try to close your
hand within a "box", that is
to say, drawing some
straight lines which correspond to the general outline
presented by your hand. As
you know, this is the "frame"
and on its correctness depends, in principle, drawing
the model well.

Fig. 299.— In order to calculate the dimensions and proportions of your fingers, of
your thumb, of your hand, try
to see the "countermould" of
the model, the hollow parts
which determine the outline
and the form of the "mould",
that is to say, the subject.

Fig. 300.— Another typical
method for calculating proportions and dimensions, in
order to construct and draw,
consists of imagining *linear
references*, horizontal lines,
that fix points or shapes that
coincide in this horizontal
scheme. Vertical or diagonal
lines which also give us the
situation, by reference, of
some points in relation to
others.

Fig. 301.— It is a question,
as you see in this last picture,
of drawing a fast sketch of
your hand in order to practise construction, the play
of light and shadow, and to
a certain extent, tonal evaluation. It would, however,
be a good idea for this study
of light and shadow and
evaluation, to draw your
hand again, this time larger
and with greater dedication,
in order to reach the same or
a similar result as in the
drawing on the following
page (fig. 302).

light and shadow, evaluation

Light paints shapes, shadow creates the volume. The light and the shade explain the shapes of objects.

In order to represent the volume we draw or paint tones or colours of different intensities or values. That is to say, we compare and evaluate some tones or shades in relation to others, we give them a value —this shade is lighter than that, this is darker than that one—. The *evaluation* is, therefore, a basic aspect both of the art of drawing and the art of painting. Corot said to Pissarro: "You are an artist and, therefore, you don't need advice, except for this. You have to study, first of all, the values. You can't paint well without them".

In order to capture the *values* of a theme, you have to know how to see, by a process of observation and comparison. the different tones that model the object. It is not a question of hundreds of shades. In reality, with just a few different greys, and black and white, it is possible to represent practically all the range of tones offered by the subject. In order to understand these problems better I invite you to draw your own left hand, with a soft lead pencil such as a 2B, just as I have done myself and as you can see in the adjoining illustration. Then try to study the factors that determine the volume of the bodies, according to the texts that accompany figure 302.

It's true that the hand is one of the most difficult subjects to draw, but I hope that the pictures and explanations on the left page will be a help to you.

Fig. 302.— The relief or volume of objects is given by the play of light and shadow, and it is important to understand their effects at the moment of drawing or painting. Here is a list of these effects:

LIGHT Illuminated parts where the colour is the *true one* of the model.

SHINE is achieved by contrast. Remember that "a white is whiter according to how dark the surrounding tone is".

"JOROBA" literally "Lump", darker part of the projected shadow between the penumbra and the reflected light.

REFLECTED LIGHT appears at the end of the shadowed part. It is more accentuated when there is a light-coloured object near the model.

PENUMBRA intermediate area between the illuminated part and the area in shadow. It is the same as "chiaroscuro" which can be defined as "light in the shadow".

REAL SHADOW all the area of shadow, opposed to the illuminated part.

PROJECTED SHADOW which appears on the surface where the object is located. Generally it is darker in the area near the object.

302

303

Fig. 303.— A reduced range of greys, limited to five or six tones, is enough to represent all the tonal values offered by the subject.

contrast and atmosphere

Evaluation, contrast and atmosphere.

The three factors, treated in the right way, create in the picture the representation of the third dimension, that is, the illusion of volume. Contrast is, moreover, an important factor in the expression and message projected by the work. El Greco, under Caravaggio's influence, accentuated the contrast to dramatize the theme of his works. Even more he surrounded the figures and the surrounds of the bodies with dark, broken down backgrounds, in order to separate his models from the background and achieve a better relief for them. He was a real *evaluator*.

In modern painting, starting from Impressionism, contrast is obtained with less aggressive, less dramatic formulas by juxtaposition of colours, which in themselves, explain the form, without the need for large, deep shadows. As Pierre Bonard said: "Colour, without any other help, is capable of explaining light, of representing shape and expressing a pictorial idea". Bonard was a real *colour man*.

In modern painters, there is, moreover, a preoccupation with representing the space by defining the foregrounds and diffusing the areas behind, thereby creating the *interposed atmosphere* as can be seen in *El palco* by Renoir (Fig. 304).

304

Fig. 304.— Auguste Renoir "El Palco". Courtauld Institute Galleries, London. An example of highlighting the depth by defining the foreground —the figure and face of the woman—, in relation to the second term —the figure of the man which is less clear and not so well finished—.

Fig. 305.— El Greco "The Resurrection of Christ". Prado Museum, Madrid.

Example of contrasts provoked by a greater relief of the figures. El Greco was one of the artists who, at that time, was influenced by the "tenebrismo" of the famous Michel Angelo Merisi, better known as *El Caravaggio*. He establishes a style of painting based on extraordinary contrasts which revolutionized the art of the baroque. Before *Caravaggio*, light was a secondary element. From then on, light, shadows, the contrast, often became important means used to express and explain the picture. Velázquez, during his first period, lived under the influence of this way of painting. El Greco also accentuated contrasts, highlighting the effect of light and shadow and the contrasts.

305

306

Fig. 306.— Here we have a practical example, a summary of the explanations on light, shadow and evaluation.

To create a sensation of space observe that the edge of the tablecloth appears blurred and diffuse.

To separate and distinguish shapes, it can sometimes be a good idea to outline the edge, as with these illuminated parts of the pear and the jug.

Provoked contrasts, reflected light, "joroba", shine, real shadow and projected shadow..., all the effects of light and shadow show up in this simple grape.

Observe the reflected lights that I have painted in the pear, in the apple and in the jug, to help create volume and highlight the form. These reflected lights existed in the model, but I accentuated them, especially in the pear, to get a more plastic effect.

The effect of the "joroba", is obvious in this fold of the tablecloth, helping to highlight its volume.

parallel and oblique perspective

In order to paint a house, a building, a street, an interior, a piece of furniture, a book, you have to know something about perspective. But it is not essential to read one of those 300 page volumes, more suitable for architects than for painters. Therefore we are going to state, in a few words, what you need to know about perspective in order to paint in oils. As you know there are three classes or forms of perspective:

1.- Parallel or vanishing point perspective.

2.- Oblique perspective or perspective with two vanishing points.

3.- Perspective with three vanishing points.

We can say that the last one is not used in artistic painting, so it will not be commented on in these texts (1).

The vanishing point or points are the place where the horizontal lines or edges of the subject meet. You will also remember that the vanishing points are always located on the *horizon line* which, in turn, is just at the height of the viewer's sight, looking ahead —you yourself, when you are painting— whether standing, sitting or bending

---

(1) For a more extensive and fuller study of perspective applied to artistic drawing and painting, I dare to recommend the book "How to draw in perspective", from the collection "Learn by doing it".

Fig. 307.— Effect of parallel or single point perspective applied to a cube and to a room.

Fig. 308.— Oblique perspective involves two vanishing points. In this case, the vanishing point on the left side remains outside the picture.

Fig. 309 and 310. Effects of parallel and oblique perspective applied to buildings and streets. Observe that for drawing figures in perspective all the heads have to be located at the height or level of the horizon line, increasing and lengthening the body according to how far away they are.

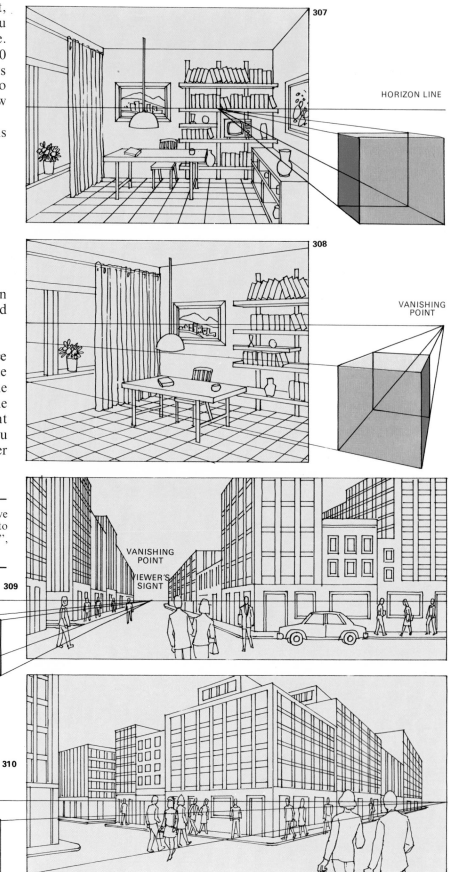

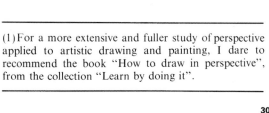

You will also remember that in parallel perspective, the only vanishing point and the centre of vision, coincide in the same place on the horizon, which does not happen with oblique perspective where the vanishing point and centre of vision are independent, still however within the horizon line.

See in the adjoining figures 307 and 309 two examples of parallel perspective, the first applied to an interior and the second to a series of buldings forming a street. The same themes appear in figures 308 and 310 resolved in oblique perspective (with two vanishing points).

Painting in oils in places where there are buildings, hamlets or just painting an urban landscape in oils, we are often faced with the problem of dividing, with correct perspective, spaces that are repeated, like for example, several doorways, windows, balconies, etc. For an expert painter, a problem of this kind is not difficult at all. It is solved simply by drawing or painting, and calculating at sight. I think it is good to know that there is a series of mathematical formulas that augment the practical knowledge. This happens when, for example, painting the facade of an old building, which has symmetrical architecture, you have to calculate the perspective centre in order to place doors and windows in the right places. It can be done at sight, but following the explanations in figures 311 to 314, it will be enough to draw an X-shaped cross and a vertical line in the centre (Fig. 312), to obtain the perspective centre, and it will be enough to complete the geometrical scheme of figure 313, to definitively indicate the position in perspective of the elements of the facade or the model.

In the adjoining figures 315 and 316, you can see a similar solution for a problem of dividing spaces in depth, applied to the facade of a country house.

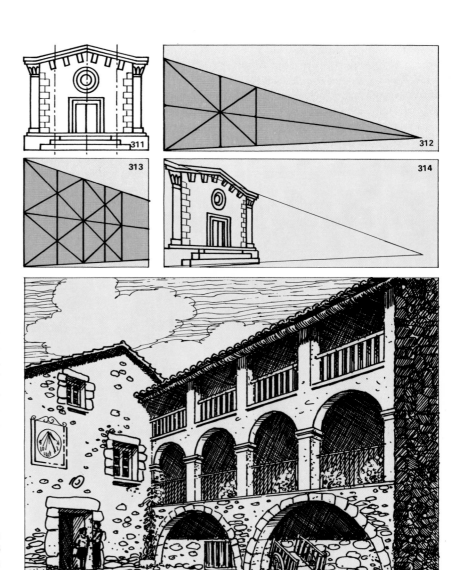

315

Fig. 311 to 314. To situate in the right perspective a building which seen from the front presents a symmetrical construction or architecture (fig. 311), it's only necessary to place in perspective the square or rectangle of the building and then divide it in two spaces in perspective, by means of an x-shaped cross.

Fig. 315.— The division of spaces in depth and in perspective may show up in old houses or rural buildings. See in the adjoining figure 316 the process to be followed in a case like this.

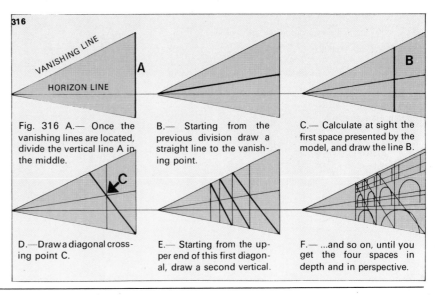

316

Fig. 316 A.— Once the vanishing lines are located, divide the vertical line A in the middle.

B.— Starting from the previous division draw a straight line to the vanishing point.

C.— Calculate at sight the first space presented by the model, and draw the line B.

D.—Draw a diagonal crossing point C.

E.— Starting from the upper end of this first diagonal, draw a second vertical.

F.— ...and so on, until you get the four spaces in depth and in perspective.

division of spaces, mosaics and guides

Schemes A, B and C in figure 317 explain how to calculate setting in perspective a certain number of equal spaces, within an also limited space. Said with pictures, given the determined space A-B, locate, in perspective five equal spaces.

On this page we offer, too, the solution of a mosaic in parallel perspective (fig. 318) and a mosaic in oblique perspective (fig. 319).

Lastly, in figure 320 and 320 A, we explain how to draw a guide of parallel lines in perspective, for those cases where the vanishing point is outside the picture.

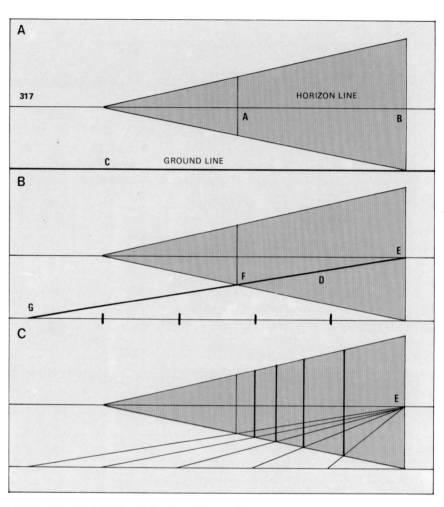

Fig. 317.— In the previous figure, number 316, we divided a space freely, without limiting ourselves to a certain measure. In this figure 317 we started from a space that had been previously determined, the same as the distance A-B. To divide this distance into, for example, five spaces, we will begin by drawing a ground line (C), parallel to the horizon line and located on the lower vertical of the perspective triangle.

B.— Then we drew the line D from point E to point F prolonging it until it crosses the ground line (point G). Then we divided the ground line in five equal spaces.

D.— Then it will be enough to draw the same number of diagonals from the previous divisions to point E to automatically get the division of spaces in depth and in perspective within a given distance.

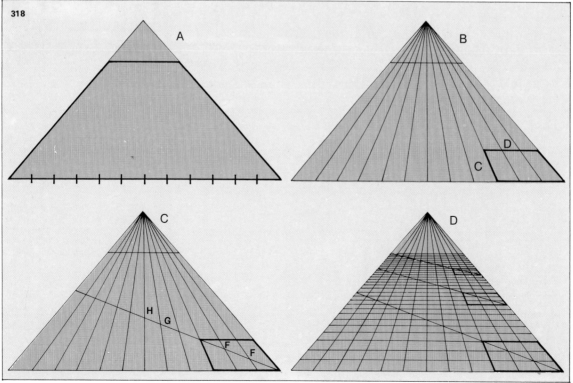

Fig. 318.— Here we have the procedure for drawing a mosaic in parallel perspective. The basis of the trick is found in the rectangle C D of the figure B, and the diagonal which appears in figure C, which give us points E F G H on the basis of which we can draw the horizontal lines that complete the mosaic in perspective.

Fig. 319.— This is the step by step development of a mosaic in oblique perspective. I hope that by studying and practising what is illustrated in these pictures, you will be able to draw it easily.

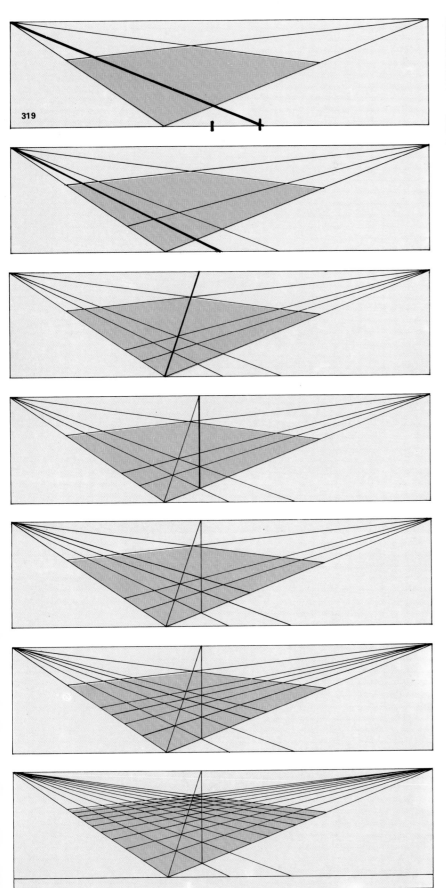

320

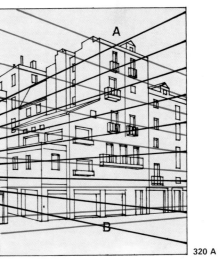

320 A

Fig. 320.— Lastly, see in this picture 320 A, the formula for calculating the perspective of a house or a building when the vanishing points are outside the picture. It's a question, as you can see, of calculating by sight the inclination of the extreme vanishing lines A and B and then dividing into a number of equal parts the two sides or lateral margins of the picture, finally drawing with hand raised, a guide with vanishing lines that allows you to draw and paint the windows, doors, balconies, moldings and projections presented by the building. The lines printed in red, locate the guide corresponding to the other vanishing point.

selecting the theme

"Irate young revolutionaries", wrote the novelist Emile Zola talking about his friends the impressionists.

Impressionism was, in fact, one of the great rebellions against decadence converted into "official art".

One of the most outstanding aspects within the impressionist revolution, was, undoubtedly, the renunciation of the big theme, the "hulk", as people called the big pictures, where the themes were chosen, studied and prepared with obvious fantasy, idealizing the model which had nothing to do with reality (fig. 321). Fighting against this traditional way of doing things, the impressionists painted in their pictures as they themselves used to say, *reasons* instead of themes, that is to say, living subjects, spontaneous scenes.

The point to be deduced from this commentary is conclusive. Selecting or finding a theme or reason for painting is not difficult at all, they exist everywhere, in your house, in the very street where you live, in the room where you are, in any village or city, garden or field.

"Themes, motives!", said Renoir, "I can get by with any buttocks whatsoever."

Neither so much nor so little. The impressionists, although they certainly confirmed their indifference for the theme, although they painted reasons so trivial as a band of workmen fixing a street (fig. 322) or a pair of old shoes (fig. 323), it's sure that beforehand they *had seen* the motif for a picture, they had thought whether the form and the colour of the motif were appropriate, that is, they had analyzed the formal and chromatic composition and had imagined how to interpret it. In reality, they had *selected the theme...* without paying much attention to the contents, whether it were a bunch of radishes or a bunch of roses.

This selection of the theme depended on them and for you it depends on three factors, which are:

1. - **Knowing how to see.**
2. - **Knowing how to compose.**
3. - **Knowing how to interpret.**

322

Fig. 322.— Claude Lorrain. (Landscape). Louvre Museum. Up unil the middle of the last century, when Impressionism began to wake up, the choice and composition of the theme was done in the artist's workshop, starting from notes and sketches drawn from the natural, but "fixing up" the theme which was made up according to the painter's vision.

323

321

Fig.s 321 and 323.— Edouard Manet. "The stonelayers in Berne street"; Butler collection. Vincent Van Gogh "Shoes"; Rijksmuseum, Amsterdam. The impressionists decided to paint motifs instead of themes. For them one didn't need to look for, and compose the theme, as their motifs were the open air, the street the most vulgar objects.

interpretation

Let's hear what Delacroix says. "My pictures are not completely real pictures. Those who simply reproduce their sketches, will never give their spectators a living feeling of Nature." It's true, the subject copied faithfully has got nothing to do with art. The primitive painters did not trace Nature. Titian, Rubens and even the classical Raphael, interpreted, much more than they copied. In their work there is a preponderance of memory work and very few direct studies have been carried out about this.

The interpretation comes, in principle, from the fact of imagining, of idealizing of "shaping in the picture the inner impressions and visions", as Picasso said.

It is easy and necessary to imagine our own picture, to see it in our own way. But the difficult thing to do, is not to lose sight of this ideal picture which every artist sees, before beginning to paint. In an interview with Pierre Bonnard, written by Angele Lamot in 1943, the famous Bonnard said: "I tried to paint some roses directly, interpreting in my own way, but I got carried away by details... and I noted that I was sinking, that I wasn't going anywhere, and that I had got lost. I could not recover my first impulse, the vision that dazzled me, my starting point." And Bonnard then gave this masterly lesson.

"The presence of the subject, of the theme, is a disturbance for the artist, while he is painting. The starting point of a picture is always an idea. The presence of the model while the picture is being carried out is a temptation and the artist runs the risk of letting himself be carried away by his direct, immediate vision, forgetting his first impulse...! And he ends up by accepting the chance, and paints details which are in front of him and which did not interest him in the beginning!" —Bonnard finishes by saying—: "Very few painters have known how to interpret the model in their own way, and those who got their own way, have their methods of self-defence."

Paul Bonnard himself then quotes Paul Cézanne as one of the few who "had his own methods of self-defence": "Cézanne had a solid idea of what he wanted to do and he only accepted from Nature what was in relation to his idea. He only accepted and painted the model as he saw it in his inmost self".

324

Fig. 324.— Paul Cézanne. "Mount Saint Victoire". Hermitage Museum, Leningrado. Cézanne painted 55 pictures of the mountain "Saint Victoire" from the window of his house, from where he could see this mountain. All of them are different, even though it is exactly the same theme. Why? Maybe because, for him, this represented the great "conquest of the model", the unusual fact of painting the model as he liked, in his own way, without letting himself be dominated by what the model "was saying"?

basic rule of the art of composition

Composing is, basically, creating.
Delacroix said: "The mind composes, that is to say, it idealizes and chooses". And —what is creating? Delacroix goes on to say, "what we call creation in great artists, is nothing more than a special way of seeing, co-ordinating and reproducing Nature".

Starting from these ideas, which it is difficult not to be in accordance with, we would have to agree with John Ruskin, in that "there are no rules about the art of composing. If there were, Titian and the Veronés would be common, and ordinary men".

Agreed. But we can and we must start from somewhere, from some standards that allow us to cultivate and perfect this "special way of seeing, co-ordinating and reproducing Nature".

One of these basic and classic rules about the art of composing, was written centuries ago by the ancient Greek philosopher, Plato, who in a few words summarized what the artist should do to order the composition of a picture. Plato simply said that:

Composing consists of finding and representing variety within a unit.

Variety in the form, in the colour, in the position and location of the elements that make up the picture, creating a diversity of forms and colours that draws the attention of the spectator and awakens his interest, which incites him to see and then gives him the pleasure of looking and comtemplating. But this *variety* should not be so great that it manages to disconcert and disperse the attention and interest created initially. That is, organizing this variety within an order and a *unity* of the whole, so that the two ideas complement each other, establishing

UNITY within the variety
VARIETY within the unity.

On this page you can see a graphic, classical explanation of these concepts, with schemes and explanations that analyze the defects and qualities of each composition.

Figs. 325, 326 and 327.— Here we have a study on the art of composing, in accordance with the basic rule of *finding and representing the unity within the variety.* See below the three schemes of these studies painted in oils, with the corresponding commentary in each case.

325

326

327

Fig. 325.— **BAD**: Excess of unity. The arrangement is not at all original, it's monotonous. See how the horizon divides the picture in two. The plate and the fruit form a single block.

Fig. 326.— **BAD**: Excess of diversity. Here the objects are dispersed, they draw attention separately, they do not lead to a reasoned, united contemplation.

Fig. 327.— **GOOD**: Correct example of *unity within the variety.* You don't have to do any more than compare this scheme with the previous ones to prove that in this one there is *unity* because of the order of the elements and diversity because of their situation.

a classic norm

When you start to paint, when the canvas is white, or rather, even before this, when the idea and the theme begin to take shape and you try to catch it in a sketch or previous drawing, an important problem about artistic composition arises, and it can be expressed in two questions: First, should I "get nearer" the theme, extending it as if I were not far away from it, or is it better to frame it "from further away", reducing the proportion of the main motif, seeing more background, etc.? and second, which would be the ideal point to locate the main element of the picture? There is no absolute norm, of course, but for these two problems —proportion and framing— there are two rules, or principles which can be followed:

1. - "Get near" the theme close enough to create a centre of interest which "explains" the contents or motif of the picture.

The second rule related to the situation of the forms within the picture is formulated by a famous aesthetic law discovered by Vitrubio, a Roman architect from the times of Augustus:

2. - The law of the Golden Section.

See this law in the adjoining box and in the commentary made on page 38 in connection with Velázquez' picture "The adoration of the Wise Kings".

Law of the golden section

Faced with a white canvas — where do you locate the main motive of a picture? In the middle, towards the top, towards the bottom, towards the right side, or towards the left? To resolve this problem the Roman architect Vitruvius established the following

Law of the golden section

So that a space divided into unequal parts turns out pleasant and aesthetic, between the smallest and largest parts there should be the same relationship as between this larger part and the whole.

In order to find this ideal division it is enough to multiply the height or the width of the canvas by the factor 0.618. (See page 38).

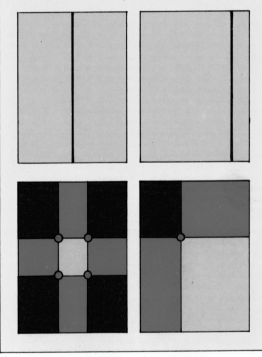

329

328

Fig. 328.— Velázquez. "The adoration of the Wise Kings". Prado Museum, Madrid. It would be too much of a coincidence that the head of the baby Jesus, is, by chance, exactly at the point where the lines of the golden section cross. We can be sure that Velázquez chose and decided on this point by applying the said principle.

Fig. 330.— Velázquez "Saint Anthony visiting Saint Paul". Prado Museum, Madrid. Is it also chance, the almost exact coincidence between the bird bringing bread to the two Saints and the point of the golden section?

330

symmetry, asymmetry

Symmetry is a synonym for *unity*. In itself it expresses order, solemnity, authority. "Symmetry is the order that appears in life whenever solemnity is needed, "said Böcklin, adding —"There is no public ceremony, no religious ceremony, without symmetry in the participants."

Trying to define symmetric composition we would say that, *it is the repetition of the elements of the picture on both sides of a central point or axis.*

Asymmetry defined as *free and intuitive distribution of the elements, balancing however, some parts in relation to others,* is a synonym of *variety*.

Choosing between one form of composition and the other, most modern artists prefer asymmetric composition, which is more dynamic and gives more opportunity to express the artist's creativity. However, it is worth the trouble to take into account, the possibility of studying in certain cases and themes, the symmetric form of composition, even rigidly, changing situations, so that, by generally accentuating the unity, the desired variety is underlined.

Figs. 331, 332.— Velázquez. "The coronation of the Virgin", Prado Museum, Madrid; and Degás. "The absent one", Impressionist Museum, Jeu de Paume, Paris. Velázquez' picture is an example of symmetrical composition, although the figures do not offer a mathematical repetition "on both sides of a central axis". Degás, in "The absent one" made a show of informal composition, moving the figures off-centre and even letting them be cut off by the frame.

331

332

schemes and balance

By a simple principle, which in art could be translated into "maximum enjoyment with a minimum effort", man prefers geometrical forms (an outline in the form of a square, circle, triangle) to abstract forms. The psychophysicist Fischer carried out a survey about this, demonstrating that most people prefer this type of simple form.

From this principle was born the idea of composing artistically, starting from basic forms or geometrical schemes like those that appear on this page (fig. 333). The first of these schemes (A), was set up by Rembrandt and makes up a classic formula of composition: a diagonal that divides the picture into two triangles.

In artistic composition, an important part is also played by *the balance of masses,* that is the fact that the "weight" of the forms is compensated by means of an off-centre axis, balancing some masses in relation to others. The Roman balance or fulcrum, is a perfect example of this balance, in relation to an off-centre axis, between an important mass or weight and a mass that weighs less.

Fig. 333.— The artistic composition of a picture may be based on geometrical schemes, just as we see in these examples. The first of these schemes, in the form of a triangle (A), is known as Rembrandt's formula.

333

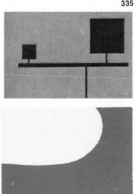

335

Figs. 334, 335. Pissarro. "The Seine at Marly". Private collection. An example of composition based on a geometrical scheme similar to Rembrandt's formula, where we also see the perfect *balance of masses* achieved by Pissarro.

334

the third dimension

Physically speaking, the picture has only two dimensions, width and height. The third dimension, *depth,* has to be imitated, and the artist has to represent it by means of forms, lights, shadows, and perspective effects. Representing the third dimension forms a part, too, of the artistic composition of a picture.

Basically, the artist can use three formulas to highlight the depth. A): *By including a foreground.* You have to select a frame which allows you to include in the foreground, a familiar shape, thanks to which the viewer can instinctively relate the size of this shape with the size of the objects situated further away. In Pissarro's picture of Dulwich College (fig. 336), there is in the foreground a tree trunk. We can see, moreover, the width of the river and its banks. These elements serve us as a reference, because of their size and their location, to mentally determine the distance and the dimensions of the building in the background, that is, they help us to create the idea of depth.

B): *By effect of perspective.* In this case it's a question of selecting an image which in itself shows a perspective effect that highlights the depth and the idea of a third dimension. In Pissarro's "New Bridge" (fig. 337), the idea of perspective and, therefore, depth is already implicit. But we must think of paths, roads, entrances to villages, and so forth where the idea is not so obvious, but equally effective.

C): *By superimposing successive planes.* When in the subject we can observe the idea of a first plane superimposed on a second plane, superimposed in turn on a third (see the adjoining figure no. 338), there is undoubtedly a possibility of representing the third dimension, just by accentuating the superimposition of shapes.

Depth can be highlighted too, by means of aerial or atmospheric perspective, remembering the principle. *The foreground is always clearer and better contrasted than the background areas.* Leonardo da Vinci said in this connection "If you finish off the far away objects with great detail, they will seem to be nearer instead of distant."

Fig. 336.— "Dulwich College". Pissarro (Collection J. A. Macaulay, Winnipeg, Canada). The third dimension is here achieved by including an outstanding foreground object (the tree trunk on the right).

336

Fig. 337.— "New Bridge". Pissarro (Collection Mr and Mrs William Coxe Wright, Philadelphia). In this case the depth is given by the vanishing of the perspective lines.

337

338

Fig. 338.— Monet "Snow in Vétheuil". (Impressionist Museum. Jeu de Paume, Paris). In this case the depth is explained by the superimposition of planes, that is, by the succession, one in front of the other, of the planes formed by the frozen river, the trees and the houses in the background.

oil painting
in practice

painting a figure in oils

In these pages we begin a series of oil painting practices, with demonstrations where, step by step, you can study the painting of two figures in oils, an urban landscape, a seascape, a country landscape and a still life. The first of these graphic demonstrations —two figures in oils—, was carried out by the renowned Barcelona artist Badia Camps.
Badia Camps has his studio in his own home. This is a room of about 3×4 m, and he always paints by daylight, with a model, and he draws every day, with charcoal or sienna or chalks, taking notes and making studies on poses, lighting, contrast, which later, in some cases, will become projects in colour and finally, definitive pictures.
But we are going to analyze in detail Badia Camps' way of painting, what he does, what he does it with, and how he does it to obtain the magnificent results you can see on these pages.
"I have thousands of drawings and sketches like these —Badia Camps told me, while showing me the sketches for figures 339 and 340—. If you were to ask me for a piece of basic advice on painting figures, I would say that you have to draw and draw again, from the natural, with a model, sketches and studies and drawings of men and women, dressed and naked, every day, until the dimensions and proportions, the anatomy, the evaluation and the contrast of the human body, are as familiar to you as taking up a pencil or brush."
For the picture that is started on this page, Badia Camps drew, as it is his custom to do, no less than five sketches, in the last of which (fig. 340), he afterwards drew, as he usually does, the rectangle that definitively frames the theme.

First stage: construction
On the white canvas, Badia Camps draws the theme directly with a brush and oil paint that is very much diluted with turpentine. For this he uses a mixture of light cobalt violet, as a basic colour, adding a little cobalt blue, natural sienna and white (figure 341). Note in this picture that, Badia Camps, following the methods of the old masters, constructs the theme with lines and tones, basically resolving the effects of light and shadow. And he does it with this violet-blue-sienna colour, similar to the colour of a neutral shadow...
Note that the construction is very carefully

339

340

Figs. 339 and 340.— Before beginning a figure picture in oils, Badia Camps draws several studies and sketches, finally marking the frame.

done as if it were —and in fact it is— a "last dress rehearsal for the work".

Second stage: painting the "base of the painting" and harmonizing the colours in general.

The way Badia Camps begins to paint, reminds me of Titian's famous "base of painting". Because, in fact, Badia Camps needs a really thick impasto of paint when beginning the picture and, like Titian he needs to take it and retake it. And this, two or three days after the "bed", when the picture has enough bite, Badia Camps goes on painting, working, forcing himself —"I have to insist, and I have to work and I have to struggle, for the emotion of painting to reach me so that I feel capable of painting"—.

341

Fig. 341.— Mixing the colours, light cobalt violet, with a little cobalt blue and a little natural sienna, diluted in abundant turpentine, Badia Camps draws and constructs the theme of the picture, with transparent lines and tones, as if he were painting with water colours.

Fig. 342.— Here we have the first phase of the "base of the painting", that is, of a first impasto, on top of which the artist will work, insist and struggle, "for the emotion of painting to reach me so that I feel capable of painting".

342

painting a figure in oils

343

Observe carefully the resolution of the picture after this second stage (figure 342). Note that it is basically the same as the initial drawing but with some slight rectifications —the size of the head is larger, for example— and observe, too, the range of warm colours, which appears in this initial stage and which is maintained until the picture is finished.

Last stage

Badia Camps takes up to ten sessions to paint a picture. After the second or third session, when the layer of paint is thick enough, half dry, sticky, Badia Camps paints in his peculiar style which he himself describes saying: "To paint in my way, I need a thick layer, a base, a bread of paint, on top of which I can apply the colours by scrubbing the brush, depositing the paint, rubbing and leaving the colour on top of the previous colour, which is dry or half dry."

Badia Camps applies the technique of "frottis"; the same as or similar to the technique used by Titian and Rembrandt.

Badia Camps' perfectionism

Badia Camps takes ten, fifteen and even more days to finish a picture. He is a perfectionist, and he is never satisfied. He has reached the extreme of rectifying and changing pictures that were already hanging in one of his exhibitions.

Fig. 343.— In this illustration of the finished pictures, the practice of the technique of "frottis" is obvious, the same technique we have talked about in connection with Titian and Rembrandt's techniques of painting (pages 38 and 36).

344

345

He is usually painting three or four pictures at the same time. The previous picture and the one I am going to comment on were painted at the same time.

Previous studies

As always, the artst first studies the picture, drawing several sketches.

Here, in these pictures (figures 344, 345) the rectification is obvious, starting first with a figure seated almost in profile, with the balcony door almost open, and a second study with the figure seen in a three-quarter position and the balcony door completely open. In the second sketch, moreover, the enhancement of the figure seems more accentuated thanks to the fact that on the left of the picture there is a dark hole between the tablecloth and the model's right arm.

The *work well done,* Badia Camps' perfectionism, is reflected here in these sketches, especially in figure 345, a finished sketch worthy of being framed.

Ready to paint, see in this chart the oil colours currently used by the artist Badia Camps.

Fig. 344 and 345.— In these previous sketches, the prelude to the picture reproduced in the following pages, Badia Camps, studies and rectifies the pose of the model and the point of view (in the right hand sketch the nearest balcony door seems open and allows us to see the shutter in the middle distance and the light from the outside).

COLOURS USED BY THE ARTIST BADIA CAMPS

Titanium white	Crimson lake
Cadmium yellow	Deep Madder
Yellow ochre	Emerald green
Raw sienna	Cinnabar green
Burnt sienna	Light violet
Umber	Light cobalt blue
Cadmium red	Prussian blue

painting a figure in oils

346

Fig. 346.— With the same mixture of colours —violet as the basic colour—, diluted with plenty of turpentine, Badia Camps draws and paints with studied precision, with lines and half-tones, as if it were a wash drawing.

Fig. 347.— Note that in this phase of the painting, when the artist is completing the first layers, the range of colours is tending towards warm, in the background there are greyish ochres and siennas, and in the tablecloth the influence of yellow and ochre is obvious.

347

First stage: construction
The same colours, and the same mixtures of colours as in the construction of the previous picture.
But observe a detail which I disregarded before. Here, and there, Badis Camps constructs by drawing, determining the forms by means of lines, he feels the worry of *adjusting, enclosing, limiting forms and outlines*.

Second stage: general harmonizing of colour.
...Here the lines and outlines disappear —"I paint by volumes" says Badia Camps—. Here we begin the "base of the painting", which for one or two sessions will provide the artist with the possibility of painting later with scrubbing or "frottis" which will personalize the style of Badia Camps.
Here too, begins his struggle to achieve a unity between the figure and the surroundings, so that the figure will not be an isolated element, out of context in relation to the background and the things that surround it. "I don't paint figures, in which case I would paint a neutral background. I paint a *theme in which a figure plays a part*". And hence the struggle to incorporate the figure into the intimate atmosphere of the room which will also form part of the picture.
At this stage he also begins the struggle to balance and harmonize the colour. "When I begin a picture, I often don't know exactly

which range of colour I'm going to use. Sometimes, as in this case, I begin with a neutral range of colour, rather warm (figure 347) and after, as the picture advances, I decide on a cold range (figure 348). In these changes I am almost always influenced by the range of colours I have on the palette. The remains of colours on the palette always represent a source of inspiration for me".

Fig. 348.— Badia Camps is now working on a thick, solid, "bed of paint" which allows him to determine the forms and colours by means of scrubbing with thick paint, just as it comes out of the tube, leaving the paint on the canvas, applying the brush gently or energetically, painting with the "frottis" technique. Study this workmanship, or way of painting, in areas such as the head, the hair-do, the blouse, the lights from the shutter in the background. Compare the general harmonization of the picture in relation to the previous stage (fig. 347), verifying that the colour tendency is bluer here, colder, and we can also see that the contrast has increased, giving the figure greater emphasis.

348

Penultimate and last stage

Between this penultimate stage (figure number 348) and the final finish (figure 349, on the following page number 168) there are few differences, but it's worth noting them. Here, on this page, the picture looks practically finished. The face the hands and feet, are not modified... And yet, most of the forms, light and shadow effects, reflections and penumbras, have been painted or touched up again, in this search for perfection, for the final touch, so dear to Badia Camps. "Without going to extremes, of course. The great problem is staying in the finish, unfinished". All right, thank you Badia Camps.

painting a figure in oils

349

painting an urban landscape in oils

Painting in the street, in the squares and avenues of the cities, in the large and small towns, in the slums, in the industrial areas, in a word, painting *urban landscapes,* is a marvellous experience. It is a classical theme and its first pictures appeared in the Renaissance and which, since then, and especially, since half-way through the last century, many artists have brought to canvas with extraordinary success. Let us just remember some impressionist painters like Pissarro, Manet, Sisley, Monet, Guillaumin, all excellent painters of the urban landscape.

I'm going to paint for you an urban landscape in oils, explaining in every detail, step by step, the process.

Here is the picture, a street in an old quarter of Barcelona, at eleven o'clock in the morning, when the light of the sun "enters" the street —note well, because this is a classical form of street illumination, with one side in shadow and the other lit by the sun.

First stage

I paint on canvas with *figure stretcher, no. 12.* To draw first stage, use a round number 10 hogs', hair brush. I prepare the colour for the initial construction. On the palette I mix Prussian blue, raw umber and ochre, diluted with quite a lot of turpentine, until I have a practically liquid paint, transparent, as if I were painting with water colours.

I draw schematically the basic lines of the houses, windows, doors, even some figures. See this initial sketch in figure 350.

Second stage

Remembering Corot and taking account of the *law of successive contrasts,* I begin by painting the shadows, with rather thin paint trying to get near the tones the model presents —a range or dark blues, with Prussian blue predominating, combined with deep madder, raw sienna and ochre (it depends on the area, whether one colour or another has more influence. See the reproduction of this second stage in figure 351). I paint without worrying and I don't mind the possibility of a mistake which, later, as the picture advances, I can rectify.

Fig. 350.— First stage: first drawing with Prussian blue and raw umber, very much diluted with turpentine, obtaining this transparent ink which allows fast drawing, as if you were painting in water colours.

Fig. 351.— "Where do you begin painting in your pictures, maestro?" Corot was asked. And the answered"- With the shadows". Certainly, the shadows create volume, explain the subject, influence the composition and show up the contrast of the picture, avoiding later optical errors, like those deriving from the *law of successive contrasts.*

350

351

painting an urban landscape in oils

Third stage

I begin the painting with the facade of the house opposite, with one basic concern, to diversify the colour of this wall with ochres, yellows, crimsons and siennas, almost always with a little blue, mixed with white. In some cases I mix the colour right on top of the canvas looking for variations which brighten and capture the reality of this prominent wall. Then I paint the side wall, the house in the background, the ground and the awnings.

All the time I am trying to enrich the shades, getting nearer to the real colour, and to the definitive form.

I worked with flat hogs', hait brushes, numbers 14, 16 and 18.

Fourth stage

I paint the sky and the clouds, remembering two basic principles;

1. - The sky is not exactly blue.
2. - On the horizon, the sky is always brighter.

In fact, Prussian blue or ultramarine blue make up the colour of the sky, according to the place where you are painting, the time of the day, whether the sky is clear or not. But as well as the blues that have been mentioned, reduced with white, we also need deep madder and sometimes raw sienna (a very small amount), to resolve the darkest part, the high part of the sky. Near the horizon, where the sky is clearer, there may be a little touch of yellow or cadmium red, or emerald green (according to the time of day). The direction of the brush-stroke in the sky need not necessarily be horizontal. In this connection the best formula is to paint without any fixed direction, "with small strokes", as Pissarro did.

In the clouds, on the other hand, when they are cumulus, as in this case, the brushstroke must be enveloping, following to a certain extent, the spherical forms of the model. Note that when merging the shadows and lights of the clouds using your fingers may be useful, but without going to extremes.

I go on with the houses in the shadow on the right side. I paint basically with Prussian blue, dark ultramarine blue, ochre, deep madder, raw sienna and emerald green, which draw definitively some of the forms of these houses.

Fig. 352.— First of all "fill" the canvas. Paint with colours that are as near as possible, most of the possible space, in order to neutralize the effect of false contrasts.

Fig. 353.— Then, once the canvas is "full", comes painting on top, constructing, adjusting forms and colours. Observe in this picture, for example, the resolution of forms and colours in the outline of the houses in shadow, on the right hand side. Good! Isn't it? and note that these are really brush strokes on a firm basis of colour painted in a previous session (figure 352).

352

353

354

Fig. 354.— This is the stage of the work where I developed a more intense and extensive labour. In the first place I painted this kind of store, on the left, which was only a question of *drawing with colours*. Afterwards I put right the effect of the perspective of the street on the left side as, if you look carefully, in the previous figure, number 353, you will be able to see that the line of the upper part (of the rooftops) does not show satisfactory perspective and, it has to lean further downwards. Lastly I squinted my eyes looking, in the subject, at this long shadow, from top to bottom, on the left side of the street, and I painted this group of blotches that represent windows, balconies, clothes hanging out, —including a lamp-post with four lamps—.

Fifth stage

I go on to paint this kind of shop or store on the left-hand side. The basis of colour painted yesterday, with quite a lot of turpentine, now allows me to paint on top of dry colours.

Then I paint the side of the house in front, lit by the sun, with this shadow lengthened from top to bottom, projected by the houses on the right-hand side. Painting this projected shadow and everything that is mixed in with it, is not easy. Here we have a complexity of shapes caused by projections, balconies, clothes hanging out and even this lamp-post with four lamps, placed in the middle of the street. So that it was only necessary to look at the model with my eyes half-closed, substituting the detailed vision for a series of blotches which, in synthesis, explained the model's complex forms.

I also had to take into account, on the other hand, the representation of space, by means of lack of contrast and definition.

painting an urban landscape in oils

Fig. 355.— Not much was left to finish the picture. The facade of the house in the centre, the ground, with the pavement in the left foreground, the outline of the houses in shadow on the right-hand side, and the figures.

I want to insist on the fact that by constructing and previously painting a basis of form and careful colours, it is relatively easy to then resolve the definitive colour and form. Look, for example, at this outline of the houses in shadow, on the right hand side of the picture. Observe the process followed from figure 352, the third stage, up to this picture of the last stage, and you will see that the first was a stain of colour, a basis of regular, uniform colour (fig. 352), then, on top of this initial basis a few simple brushstrokes of colour were added (fig. 353); and finally, in this last demonstration, a little more was constructed, —very little— a few colours were painted —very few— the final effect is achieved. It is a problem of synthesis, which I ask you to analyze in the whole progress of this picture.

355

Last stage

Now I only have to complete the finish of the facade of the centre house, and the ground and some forms of the house in shadow on the right, and the figure too. These have to be constructed and painted from memory, with certain reference with respect to the subject, trying to retain the positions of the people who are walking along the street, and the colours, as well as the light and shade effects they show. I construct and paint these figures with care and attention, but without pretending to an excessively formal finish which would not be in keeping with the general feeling of the picture.

And I have finished

Before signing it, with the picture already at home, in the studio, it is a good idea to go over what you've done, a few hours later, in case you need to touch up something —which you always have to.

painting a seascape in oils

Here we have another traditional theme painted by many artists all over the world and especially in those countries which border the sea, like England and Spain, offering extensive thematic material that includes everything from the fishing port of a small village on the coast, with its boats, beacons, nets and buoys, to the frame of a corner of a large city port... passing through beaches with figures, surges of waves, boats at sea coves and cliffs. This last theme, the cliff of a beach on the Costa Brava, in Cataluña, in the town of Lloret de Mar, is going to be the subject of this demonstration of how to paint a seascape in oils.

I have to say that when I contemplated this picture for the first time, I immediately associated the form of the rocks with cubes, parallelepipeds and pyramids, with geometrical forms, and I must add that before beginning the picture it seemed essential to me to draw stones and rocks formed by cubes, parallelepipeds and pyramids. Here are these drawings, as an exercise before painting a seascape with rocks and cliffs, painted on the Costa Brava of Cataluña.

First stage:

I begin by quickly sketching, schematically, the complexity of the cliff made up of numerous projections and groups of rocks.
On the palette I have made up a bluish grey colour basically of Prussian blue and a little raw umber. I mix these colours with a lot of turpentine, to paint with a transparent colour which lets the brush move quickly and draw uninterrupted lines.
While I'm doing it, and as this initial scheme is being drawn, it may be interesting to sketch the basic shadows of the model, trying, in a first attempt, to approach too the basic colour shown by the model with a bluish tendency in some cases, a sienna tendency in others.
I painted the lineal parts with a round hogs hair number 8 brush and the Shadowed parts with a flat number 12 hogs' hair brush.

Second stage:

In this second stage I will try to paint the basic colour of the sea and the sky. I'll work with flat, number 16 and 18 hogs hair brushes.

356

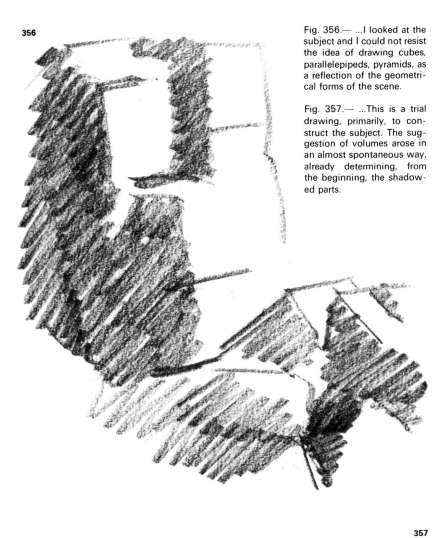

Fig. 356.— ...I looked at the subject and I could not resist the idea of drawing cubes, parallelepipeds, pyramids, as a reflection of the geometrical forms of the scene.

Fig. 357.— ...This is a trial drawing, primarily, to construct the subject. The suggestion of volumes arose in an almost spontaneous way, already determining, from the beginning, the shadowed parts.

357

painting a seascape in oils

I paint the sea. In the sea there is Prussian blue, ultramarine, burnt umber and a little crimson, as well as white. In the sea there is also a little madder. Basic rule, the brush strokes in the sea have to be horizontal. But in some areas, due to the currents caused by the channel over the rocks (foreground and left part of the finished picture) the waves come towards us diagonally. In these areas we may have to change the direction of the brush strokes to this same diagonal movement. Except in the darkest areas of the sea, in the foreground, white always intervenes to brighten the blue. But a very small amount.

Third stage:

This is a picture to be completed in several sessions with the technique of *painting by stages.* A laborious theme, which has to be done with good, careful construction, and which therefore demands to be painted and

358

359

Figs. 358, 359.— The two stages of this seascape painted in oils, graphically explain the idea of how and where to begin a picture: *Covering up the white of the canvas as soon as possible,* would be the right response. That is to say, first drawing the basic lines of the picture, but staining, in a first attempt, the shadowed parts which create volume (figure 357); "covering" immediately the sky and the sea (figure 358), which means the picture begins to live, to approach reality, and painting quickly the group of rocks —lights and shadows—, with paint that has been diluted with a lot of turpentine, so that it dries quickly and lets you repaint, *beginning the real picture* (figure 359).

360

repainted, in successive stages, to represent the volume, to paint and draw the complicated form of the rocks, the waves and the foam on the water.

Therefore it's normal that now, when I am going to paint the illuminated parts of stones and rocks, I should do it with paint that is still thin, still with a certain amount of turpentine, so that it dries more quickly and tomorrow I can paint on top with greater security and cleanliness.

I paint the illuminated colours of stones and rocks, trying to get as near as possible to the colours of the subject (see the finished picture on page 177, fig. 362).

Fourth stage:

Now it's a question of definitively resolving the drawing and painting of the rocky forms, situated in the middle distance.

On the other hand I think that this could be a monotonous, grey theme, without much interest... and that to make it pleasant, alive, and interesting, I need carefully to interpret the colour, trying to see colours, —a lot of colours in the illuminated parts, in the shadowed parts, everywhere. And this is what I'm doing in this session, working unhurriedly, trying to see the tone which is always different, applying the colour with flat wide brushes, numbers 12 to 18.

Fig. 360.— What follows is now a question of *work well done,* of painting looking at the scene, carefully copying forms and colours, although still trying to diversify and enrich the colour, contrasting, accentuating, analyzing in each case. Asking myself if I can improve them. Here I dedicated my efforts to the rocks in the middle distance.

painting a seascape in oils

361

Fifth stage:

I am working on the two hills in the background, on the left, following on with the previous technique of direct painting, painting now with less brilliant colours than in the middle distance, greying and diffusing, to create a feeling of space, in order to represent the distance, and the atmosphere between.

Sixth and last stage:

At last I paint the sky and the sea.

I brighten the colour of the sky on the left, thus managing to outline the silhouettes of the hills, and on the right hand side I paint some clouds, in a luminous spring sky.

The colour of the sea is basically made up of Prussian blue, ultramarine and white, but burnt umber, madder, yellow ochre and emerald green also play a larger or smaller part. Yellow ochre and burnt umber, when mixed with Prussian blue or ultramarine and white, give a broken sea blue, more or less blue according to the proportion of ochre and burnt umber, which all together resolve the colour of the water.

The construction and the waves and the foam when the water breaks against the rocks, has to be resolved by looking at the scene, the movements and play of the water, studying the forms and colours for a few minutes, and then painting from memory, directly, interpreting what you remember.

Lastly, in the foreground, I have tried to create the maximum contrast of forms and colour, trying to "get nearer", to better represent the foreground.

Figs. 361, 362.— The process set out in the previous figure continues, applied to the group of rocks and hillocks in the background —where there is a preoccupation to make it greyer, dissipate and diffuse, paying attention to the atmospheric

362

effects, then painting the rocks in the foreground, where you can see my struggle to achieve a maximum contrast of form and colour, then working on the sky. Finally I propose painting the sea, the waves and the foam of the water where it breaks against the rocks, an element of the picture which has to be painted from memory, observing attentively, for a while, the form and the colour of the foam.

painting a seascape in oils

It was five o'clock in the afternoon one day in September, when this effect against the light surprised me, at an altitude of almost a thousand metres, in the middle of the mountainside, in Montseny, in Cataluña. I decided to make a quick sketch with a 5B lead pencil, (Fig. 363). The result looked hopeful to me, and then I went on to paint an oil sketch, for which I used a canvas cardboard no. 1, figure. The previous study of a theme by means of sketches and colour notes, forms part of the normal work of an oil painter. This sketch, this note, represent the opportunity for better identification with the theme, as well as a general trial that allows us to evaluate the possibilities of the theme as an artistic picture. Painting the same theme twice, three times, is good. Great artists like Cezanne, in the Mont *Saint-Victoire,* Manet in his cathedrals, Picasso, in his series on the artist and the model, did so. In the last instance, a note of colour beforehand means painting the final picture with better understanding of the cause and with greater enthusiasm.

It was like this, in my case. I selected a canvas with a frame, no. 30 landscape and I began to paint.

First stage (fig. 365)

With charcoal, I draw happily and vigorously, as can be seen in figure 365, but calculated, well constructed, even calculated with plays of light and shadow, knowing that later, at the first painting session, I will erase and destroy all these details and tonal shade, but knowing too, that this study remains in the memory, and influences the construction of the picture.

Second stage (fig. 366)

I begin to paint. I try to cover the canvas with a minimum of colours, the luminous green of the meadow, the dark green of the trees, the mountains in the background, the sky...
Note that for the present I have not bothered to conserve some branches of trees, and even the two trees on the right, which are now covered by the sky and which later I will paint on top of this light blue. This is, to sum up, a stage in which the picture is resolved in large masses, in a very primitive way, but with bases which allow us to paint and repaint on top.

363

364

Fig. 363, 364.— It is always profitable to first study a theme, by means of sketches and even with a note of colour. You have the chance to really study the frame, the form, the contrast, the colour.

Fig. 365.— A landscape like this, where the form is just as important as the colour, and is heightened by the against-the-light effect, seemed to me should be first drawn with charcoal, studying values, foregrounds and backgrounds.

Fig. 366.— Stain, stain! The first thing is to cover the canvas with a layer or base of colour which then lets us develop the picture.

painting a landscape in oils

Figs. 367, 368.— Among the advice Ingres gave his pupils there is something we should not forget. He says "A good picture is the one which at any moment can be considered finished. When it's just a drawing, when one is beginning to paint, when it's half done..." and he added—: "Don't stay stuck in one place in the picture, draw and paint everything at the same time, go over the canvas, make the picture progress always at the same time, all of it at the same time".

While I was painting this landscape I remembered and tried to follow Ingres's advice. And I believe that I was able to fulfil it thanks to the sketches I made before beginning to paint. On the basis of these I became familiar with the theme. For me it was easier to "go over the pictures".

367

368

painting a landscape in oils

369

Third stage (fig. 367)

I begin this third stage, adjusting the colour of the sky, brightening the area which borders on the horizon. I heighten the white of the clouds on the right. I paint again the mountains in the background, enriching the colour. I sketch the trunks of the two oaks in the right middle distance and I paint the fir tree in the middle distance.

I paint some small branches on these vertical trunks and then I go on to the Canadian pine in the centre. The construction of this pine compels me to repaint the small areas or "holes" through which the colour of the sky appears.

Fourth stage (fig. 368)

I paint the two small oaks, a slow job where one is subject to what the subject "says", I continue with the burnt or dead tree, ochre-red in colour, just in front of the fir tree. I paint trunks in the little wood on the left, and I "open" lights in the ground and in the background.

Fifth and last stage (fig. 369)

Now it's a question of reconstructing, first, the little wood on the left, painting and repainting trunks, "opening" lights in the lower part, opening too "holes" between the foliage of the trees, to represent the interstices through which we can see the sky. I add colour to the dark foliage, with a mixture of Prussian blue, raw sienna and ochre. Then I paint the lights of grass and plants near the fence, in the middle of the picture. I paint the areas of earth in the green meadow, and the shadows caused by the trees on the left-hand side and, lastly I paint again all the green meadow, producing slight differences in colour, adding little white and red flowers.

Fig. 369.— There are considerable differences between this picture and the previous one. The radial shadows of the tree trunks are somewhat brighter in colour. The colour of the earth in the foreground is more lively and in the branches and leaves of the trees there are some green shades trying to illuminate and create volume. The whole area of the wood (left hand side of the picture) has been reconstructed both insofar as concerns the colour and the form. Lastly I have painted the grass again, diversifying the colour, adding little flowers. Apart from these changes, there are the added changes of forms and colours that did not appear in previous stages. This has to be the final work of a picture.

painting a still life in oils

370

371

This last demonstration on how to paint a still life, will at the same time be a practical lesson, an exercise that I offer you and which I beg you to carry out—, as a summary of the teaching from this book. The still life is, according to what Van Gogh said in one of his letters to his brother Theo: *"the best model for learning to paint"*. The still life, on the other hand, allows us to paint at home, without witnesses, with all the comforts and advantages that this offers. There are, moreover, previous histories, samples, hundreds of reproductions of still lifes painted by great masters which can help you to select the subject, to compose, to determine the lighting.

Here, for example, in figure number 370, we have a still life that I composed in the style of Cézanne, the great impressionist master of still life. Note that, following Cézanne's lesson, I have arranged a plate of fruit and a vase, a tumbler and further fruit, on a rumpled white tablecloth, on a table that is partly uncovered. This was Cézanne's favourite formula in all his still lifes (figure 371). Well —do it yourself! Try to find a vase like Cézanne's somewhere in your house, buy some fruit, put it all on a tablecloth... and paint!

372

Fi. 370.— Photograph of the model

Fig. 371.— Paul Cézanne. "Still life of the curtain" (fragment). Museum of the Hermitage. Leningrado.

Fig. 372.— Begin with a well adjusted drawing, which can be done in charcoal, with lines only, for the moment.

First stage: initial construction
Size of the picture a 25 figure canvas. Draw the theme with charcoal. First make some smaller-sized sketches, with lead pencil or charcoal or chalk, studying the shapes and values.

painting a flower in oils

But let me take a brief pause.

In the still life that you and I are painting, there is a flower, a rose. Flowers are a very appropriate theme for an oil painting. But there are people who think that painting flowers is difficult, both because they haven't a concrete form, —I'm talking about roses, iris, gardenias, that is, about flowers which like daisies, don't offer us a geometrical form—, and because they have to be painted fast, freshly cut, before they lose the beauty of the first day.

In the first place we are going to clear up the idea that drawing a rose is more difficult than drawing a hand and that the same teaching on fitting in, "counter mould" and points of reference that appears on page 146, are perfectly applicable to the drawing and construction of a rose. And let's say too that painting a rose is no more difficult than painting an apple, as you can see in the examples in this chart.

Fig. 373.— J. M. Parramón. "Crystal vase of flowers". Private collection. Flowers are an excellent subject, but they have to be painted in one day, in one or two sessions, so that they don't change shape, or wilt.

373

How to paint a flower

Fig. 374. First I advise you to draw the form of the flower as perfectly as possible. Starting from this very accurate drawing, here is the process I followed while painting this example.

374

375

376

377

Fig. 375. First I painted the background, then a dark green on the leaves and lastly a dark red or crimson, with hardly any variations, on the general form of the flower, which may seem contradictory because it covers and eliminates the initial drawing, but it's certain that this initial drawing helps us to remember forms, which we can resolve by painting and drawing at the same time.

Fig. 376. Notice in this picture, where, painting with bright colours on top of the dark crimson background, I have basically modelled the form of the petals.

Fig. 377. This is the final result with the same system applied to the leaves. Observe the following important details. In this last phase I used the background colour again to outline and to fade away shapes. On the flower, as well as deep madder, red and white, I used Prussian blue and burnt umber.

painting a still life in oils

The first stage continues. Study of lights and shadows (figure 378)

After the short aside on how to paint a flower, we continue with the first stage of the still life, confirming the construction, and at the same time, studying the masses or blotches that determine the scheme of the picture. Once this drawing is finished, also done in charcoal, we have to fix it with a special spray for charcoal.

Second stage (fig. 379)

I begin the picture trying to stain and cover the canvas, painting the background colours, the grey areas of the cloth, the dark sienna of the table... in order to eliminate the large white spaces and better adjust the colours of the subject.

Third stage (figure 380, following page number 185)

See the illustration on the following page, the state of the picture once the first colouring phase is completed, after covering, as a start, all the canvas.

We are in the middle of the development of the picture, but there are already some elements, in the folds of the cloth, in the background, which can be considered definitive.

On the other hand, there are aspects such as the form of the bunch of grapes, which will go on evolving and changing until the end, with laborious work of construction and even correction.

It is notable, apart from this, the fact that up until this third stage I had painted one peach less and a different apple. Compare this illustration with the photograph in figure 370, page 182).

Fourth stage (figure 381)

It seemed to me that I could add a peach to the background, and that I needed to change the apple in the foreground, which I did from this fourth stage onwards.

All the fruit is practically completed insofar as concerns form and colour in this phase, except for the bunch of grapes which still appears confused and badly constructed. In this, and in every case, we have to follow literally what the subject "says". It is not a good thing to improvise or to paint from memory. A bunch of grapes is something complex which forces us to copy exactly the forms and colours presented by the fruit.

378

379

Fig. 378.— I believe that a complete initial construction, drawing first lineally, as I did in figure number 372, and later finishing the drawing with a study of lights and shadows, as I have done here, is very helpful, in the case of a still life like this one.

Fig. 379.— As always, the first preoccupation is to cover up the whiteness of the canvas, to avoid optical effects caused by false contrasts.

380

Fig. 380.— First attempt at colour, with not much impasto yet, sticking to the drawing and the structure of the previous stage. The paint already covers the whole canvas and at this moment it seems obvious that we need to carry out some changes in the group. In the first place, the apple in the left foreground offers a not very easily identifiable form, it is small and its shape is not typical. In the second place the three fruit on the plate, together with the grapes, are very similar in colour and form, they offer no *variety*. The arrangement of the grapes also sins by excess of *unity*, and lastly, in the background, near the back of the chair, I miss something, I find the space empty. Well, all these defects can be corrected, as long as one does not paint like an automaton. One should think, analyze, contemplate, criticize and change, if necessary.

painting a still life in oils

Fig. 381.— Here is the solution to the problems set out in the previous condition, a typical apple in the left foreground, three items of fruit in the dish, and also reconstruction of the grapes, and a peach added in the background, near the back of the chair.

The picture appears here one stage nearer to the end. There are some elements which can already be considered finished, like the three items of fruit in the dish and the peach in the background. The grapes will be reconstructed again and glass of wine, the vase and the rose will be painted directly during the last session.

(Note: This phase of the picture was reproduced photographically, with the paint still wet, so in the reproduction there are reflections and glints off the paint).

Fig. 382.— In this last stage the work was certainly laborious, beginning by reconstructing and definitively painting the bunch of grapes, painting the rose completely the vase and the glass, repainting the background, the bare table in the foreground, and the tablecloth. All of this on top of the first stages painted previously, which allowed me to go back again to aids and supports created by myself.

Observe the basic colour of the tablecloth, grey in this fourth stage, ready for me to paint in the lights and shadows which will determine the wrinkles and the whiteness of the original. (compare this fourth stage with the finished picture on the following page).

Fifth and last stage (figure 382)
I painted this picture in four sessions of two hours each. Are you going to paint a still life during the next weekend? It would be the best lesson of all those I've tried to give you in this book.

glossary

A

Acrylic, paint. Acrylic colours, basically made up of synthetic resins, a product of modern technology. They were adopted in artistic painting from the sixties, onwards. They are sold in tubes, as a fluid paste similar to oil colours. Acrylic colours offer a certain similarity to colours that are soluble in water (water colours and tempera), with the peculiarity that the freshly applied, still damp colour, is soluble in water, but when it's dry it's practically indelible.

Alla prima. Italian expression which can be translated by "at the first try". It's used to mean the technique of direct painting which resolves the painting in a single session, without previous preparation or later stages.

Asymmetry. Free and intuitive distribution of the elements of a picture, but still balancing some parts in respect to others.

B

Balsam, Canada. Raw resin used in varnishing. It comes from the resinous exudate of a tree from the conifer family.

Base of the painting. Initial draft of the picture, painted with a relatively thick layer —half impasto—, on the basis of which Titian began the real picture.

Binder. Liquid products such as drying oils, solvents, resins, balsams, waxes, etc., used to bind colours or pigments finely ground in the manufacture of oil colours.

Bite. State of a layer of paint when it is almost dry, is slightly sticky, but lets you paint on top with thin impastos, light colours, rubbing, offering a certain resistence and softness which can condition and improve the workmanship of the picture.

Bitumen Judea. Asphalt, a tarry compound, dark brown in colour, used in the 17th and 18th centuries for oil painting. It is shiny and has a warm attractive tone. But the fact that it never dries completely has been the cause of deterioration and imperfections in pictures painted at that time.

C

Canvas-covered cardboard. Cardboard covered with canvas for painting on, and bound. Canvas-covered cardboard is available in the sizes indicated in the international stretcher table, up to number eight.

Carbon, pencil. For drawing with lines and softness. With similar characteristics to a lead pencil, it has several different names: "Conté pencil", "París pencil", "Carbon pencil", "compound carbon pencil". The lead is *composed* of vegetable carbon as the basic material and it gives a finer, more fixed line than charcoal.

Cardboard. Thick sheet made of wood pulp, usually grey in colour, used as a support for oil painting. Often the preparation for painting on a piece of cardboard, is carried out just by scrubbing it with raw garlic.

Cartoon. A reduced drawing or plan for a mural painting or a tapestry.

"Cat's tongue". Popular term used to describe the filbert brush, which is flat with a rounded end.

Cenital. Diffuse light which reaches the model from the upper part of the place where the subject is.

Chalk. Cylindrical or square stick which colours by rubbing. It is made up of powdered earths, ground with oils, water and other substances. Chalk is similar to pastels, but it is more stable and gives a harder line. There are chalks that are white, black, light sienna, dark sienna, cobalt blue and ultramarine blue.

Charcoal. Thin, carbonized branch of willow, hazel or rosemary, used for drawing, generally sketches.

Chiaroscuro. Those parts or areas of the picture which, even though they are in shadow, however intense it is, allow the model to be seen. It can be defined as the art of painting light in shadows. Rembrandt was one of the great masters of the chiaroscuro.

Colour, local. It is the real colour of objects, in those parts where it is not modified by effects of light and shade or by reflected colours.

Colour, reflected. It is a constant factor, taking into account on the one hand, the colour of the surroundings, and on the other the concrete reflection of one or more objects.

Colour, tonal. This is a colour that varies to a greater or lesser extent from the local colour, generally influenced by the reflection of other colours.

Complementary colours. Speaking in terms of *light colours,* complementary colours are secondary colours which only need one primary to make up and white light (or vice versa). Example: when yellow —made up of the light colours green and red— is added to blue, white light is recomposed.

Cotton, canvas or linen. Cloth designed to support oil paint as a substitute for linen canvas or cloth. In comparison with linen canvas, cotton canvas has a lighter colour, less compact weave and is more economical. Some manufacturers dye the cotton cloth, imitating the colour of the linen cloth.

Cracked. Fractures or splits that appear in impastos and layers of oil paint, when the old rule of painting "fat over lean" has not been observed. See the entry "fat over lean"

D

Dammar. It is one of the most frequently used resins in making varnishes to be applied to oil paint. It comes from certain trees of the conifer family. It is soluble in benzol and in petrol. It dissolves well in alcohol and in turpentine.

Dippers. Small containers, usually metal, for holding liquid solvents, turpentine and linseed oil. The classic model consists of two small metal vessels, with a spring or clip on the base that can be used to attach them to the edge of the palette. There are also individual dippers, with just one container.

E

Emulsion. Liquids, in the form of microscopic particles, suspended in other liquids, without mixing. Example: the emulsion for tempera painting made up of distilled water and egg yolk. The egg yolk keeps the oil and the acqueous and albuminous mixture of the yolk in a stable suspension.

at over lean. Oil paint is *fat;* diluted with turpentine it is *lean.* When, by mistake, lean is painted over fat, the lean layer dries more quickly than the fat, and when the latter is dry, the one on top contracts and cracks.

Fauvisme. Term of French origin derived from the word *fauve* applied for the first time by the critic Vauxcelles talking about an exhibition that took place in 1905 in the Autumn Salon in Paris. The *fauve* movement was headed by Matisse and also included Derain, Vlaminck, Marquet, Vandongen, Dufy, etc.

Ferrule. In a brush for painting, the ferrule is the metallic part which holds the hairs.

Filbert. Term used to distinguish flat brushes with a rounded point, commonly known by the name "cat's tongue".

Frottage. (Scrubbing). Term derived from the French verb *frotter* (to rub), used in painting with a technique that, basically, consists of lightly loading the brush with thick paint, and painting by scrubbing on top of an area that has already been painted and is dry or almost dry. It is generally used with light colours on top of dark colours.

G

Glaze. Transparent layer of oil paint applied to an area of the picture, with the aim of modifying a colour that has already been painted.

Grey, optical. (1) The effect achieved by means of light glazes on top of a dark background, which can be compared with a drawing done on a black blackboard, with plaster chalk spread out with your fingers; which promotes a series of grey graduations which, later, when local colours are applied, goes on showing through, forming the classical "optical greys".
(2) The terms "optical greys" and "optical blacks" are applied also to mixtures of the three primary colours yellow, magenta and cyan which can be adjusted to form a final colour without hue. Similar optical colours may be obtained by mixing one primary with the appropriate secondary colour which amounts to the same thing as mixing three primaries.

Grisaille. Painting carried out with white, black and greys, imitating low relief sculptures. It is often used in studies and sketches for sculptures. By extension, we talk of painting grisailles when there is an abundance of greyish shades in the picture or part of it.

I

Impasto. Thick, dense, covering layer of oil paint. Characteristic way of painting, with the brush loaded and leaving a considerable amount of paint on the canvas.

Induction of complementary colours. This is explained by saying that "to modify a certain colour it is enough to change the background colour that surrounds it".

L

Lead, for pencils. Term used to mean a common pencil made up of cedar wood and a "lead" composed of graphite and slate.

Linen. Textile cloth used to make canvases for oil painting. It can be distinguished by its rigidity and somewhat dark ochre grey colour. It is considered to be the best cloth for oil painting.

Linseed oil. Drying oil for oil painting, extracted from flax seeds. It is used to thin oil paint, usually mixed with turpentine.

M

Mahl stick. Thin stick, about 70 or 80 cm. long, topped by a small ball, used to rest the hand holding the brush on, when painting small areas, so as not to mark the rest.

Medium. Solvent for oil paint composed of a mixture of synthetic resins, drying varnishes and solvents that evaporate slowly or fast. As a traditional medium that one can prepare oneself, we recommend a mixture of equal parts of linseed oil and rectified turpentine.

Motif. This is the modern definition of the "theme" introduced by the Impressionists, to mean a model without any apparent preparation, just as it appears in daily life.

Mummy. An oil colour with similar characteristics to those of bitumen of Judea (see this entry).

P

Palette. Surface for arranging and mixing colours. They are rectangular or ovaloid, and the most commonly used are made of wood although there are some made of plastic and of paper. The term *palette* is used too, to refer to the colours used by a painter.

Panel. Term used to mean wood used as a support for oil painting, tempera, acrylics, etc. In ancient times they used the wood of white poplar in Italy of oak, in Flanders and of oak, beech, walnut, cedar or chestnut in Spain. At present the favourite is mahogany.

Perspective. This is the science that graphically represents the effects of distance on the appearance of size, form and colour. We can distinguish between lineal perspective, which represents the third dimension or depth by means of lines and forms, and aerial perspective, which represents depth by means of colours, tones and contrasts.

Pigments. Pigments are all those ingredients which, when ground in a binding medium, provide a colour for painting. Pigments for painting are generally in the form of powder and can be organic or inorganic.

Poppy oil. It comes from the seeds of the opium poppy, and is mainly used in the manufacture of oil colours. It is a suitable oil for painting glazes.

Primary colours. Basic colours of the solar spectrum. *Primary light* colours are blue, green and red; *primary pigment* colours are yellow, magenta and cyan blue.

Priming. Layer of plaster and glue applied to the cloth, cardboard or wood, as a preparation for oil painting.

glossary

R

Repentance. Term used when an important part of the picture is modified and reconstructed, signifying that the artist regrets what he has already painted. Velázquez's *examples of repentance* are well known, and have been discovered in modern times by infra-red rays.

Resin. Gummy substance coming from certain plants, which hardens on contact with air. It is used to make varnishes in the manufacture of oil paints.

S

Sable, hair. Sable hair brushes are used in oil painting as auxillaries to hogs' hair brushes. A sable hair brush is soft and offers less resilience to touch. It is suitable for retouching, painting thin lines, small forms and details.

Sacking. canvas or cloth of. Cotton cloth with a very thick weave, used as a support for oil paint on certain occasions. Sacking takes broad workmanship, suitable for large murals painted in oils.

Sanguine. Square stick of chalk of a reddish sepia colour, with similar characteristics to pastels, but more compact and harder. Sanguine is a procedure for drawing by rubbing with similar techniques to carbon and pastel. It is also available in pencil form.

Scale. (Range).

Secondary colours. Colours of the spectrum made up of the mixture in pairs, of the primary colours. The *secondary light* colours are cyan blue, magenta and yellow. The *secondary pigment* colours are red, green and blue.

Sfumato. Italian term applied to Leonardo da Vinci's painting as he recommended and practised blurring the outlines of the model.

Siccative (dryer). Solution added to oil colours to make them dry more quickly. It is not a good idea to add an excessive amount, because it prejudices the conservation of the painting.

Simultaneous contrast. Optical effect according to which a colour is darker to the extent that the colour surrounding it is lighter, and vice versa. On the other hand, the juxtaposition of two different tones, of the same colour, promotes the exaltation of both tones, brightening the bright one and darkening the dark one.

Soaked in. Part or area of a canvas where the layer of paint appears matt, next to shining parts or areas, because the oil or varnish has been absorbed or because of the action of turpentine.

Spanish white. The common name given to the plaster made up of natural calcium carbonate, which is used mixed with glue, to size cloth, as the preparatory basis of the surface that is going to be painted on.

Split colours. Also called broken colours. Colours made up of the mixture of two complementary colours in unequal proportions plus white.

Squirrel hair. Squirrel hair brushes are, too, auxillaries to hogs' hair brushes for oil painting. Squirrel hair (of animal origin like sable) is rather softer and has slightly less resilience than sable hair. It fulfills the same mission and is cheaper.

Stretcher. Wooden frame that can be taken apart, with special characteristics, on which we mount the cloth we are going to paint on.

Stretcher-carrier. A piece of equipment made up of two strips of wood, each with two metallic angles and two screws, which, mounted on two stretchers with canvas, keep the surfaces of the two canvases separated, allowing a freshly painted canvas to be carried around without being stained of spoilt.

Successive pictures. Rule established by the physicist Chevreul according to which "the vision of any colour whatsoever creates by sympathy the appearance of the complementary colour".

Support. Any surface whatsoever on which a pictorial work can be carried out. Examples: canvas, panels, paper, cardboard, walls, etc.

Symmetry. This is related to artistic composition and is defined as "the repetition of the elements of the picture on both sides of a central point or axis".

T

Tacks. Small very sharp nails, with a wide, flat head, used to attach the canvas to the wooden stretcher. Nowadays this is often done with metal staples.

Tempera. One of the oldest painting procedures, already used in the 12th century and widely described in the 14 and 15th by Cennino Cennini. It is characterized by the use of egg yolk as a solvent and binder for the coloured earths.

Tertiary colours. Series of six *pigment colours* obtained by mixing primary and secondary colours in pairs. The tertiary pigment colours are, orange, scarlet, violet, ultramarine blue, emerald green and light green.

Turpentine. Oil free of fat, volatile, commonly known as *turpentine,* used as a solvent in oil painting. Mixed in equal parts with linseed oil, it supplies a classic *medium,* as thinner on its own it gives ri to a matt finish.

V

Value. The relationship existing between the differen tones of one picture. To evaluate is the same as comparing and resolving the effects of light and shadow b means if different tones.

Varnish for protection. Is the varnish applied to the picture to protect it, once it is finished and dry. The protective varnish is now on sale in bottles and in aerosol sprays and can be matt or glossy.

Varnish for retouching. Use t retouch areas of the picture where the paint seems matt, unlike the rest which is gloss These differences in shine als suppose differences in colour which are eliminated with the retouching varnish.

"Verdaccio". Oil colour used by the ancient masters in the first phase or construction of the picture, applied with solvent. "Verdaccio" was a mixture of black, white and ochre.

W

Walnuts, oil of. This is a solvent for oil painting, coming from the pressing of ripe walnuts. Very liquid, slow drying, and indicated for painting styles that demand thin lines, outlines and detailed finishes.

Wax, colours. Basically made up of pigments and colours bound with wax and fatty materials, melted with heat at high temperatures, forming a homogeneous paste which once it is dry, is usually in cynlindrical forms. They are stable colours, they colour by rubbing and cover up to a certain point, allowing a light colour to be applied on top of a dark colour and lightening it by mixing with it.

Wedge. Small triangles of wood, about five millimetres thick, which are used as wedges in the four corners of a stretcher, in order to pull the canvas tight.